SQUARE UP

50,000 miles in search
of a way home

LISA DAILEY

Sidekick Press
Bellingham, Washington

This memoir represents the author's recollection of her past. These true stories are faithfully composed based on memory, photographs, diary entries, and other supporting documents. Some names, places, and other identifying details have been changed to protect the privacy of those represented. Conversations between individuals are meant to reflect the essence, meaning, and spirit of the events described.

Published 2021
Printed in the United States of America
ISBN: 978-1-7344945-5-6
LCCN: 2020952538

Sidekick Press
2950 Newmarket Street, Suite 101-329
Bellingham, Washington 98226
sidekickpress.com

Lisa Dailey, 1973-
Square Up: 50,000 Miles in Search of a Way Home

Cover design by: HL Creatives

Dedicated to the three sides of my square:
Ray, RJ, and Tyler

PROLOGUE

The notion that bad things happen in threes is bullshit. I was thirty-five the summer my father died. I hadn't seen him in years. Cal, my maternal grandfather, died three short months later. As leaves changed from green to orange, it seemed even the trees mourned. As a new year began, holding promise for new beginnings, my twenty-three-year-old brother, Zack, overdosed just as he was gaining a foothold in sobriety. Still reeling from the death of Zack, our mother was diagnosed with an aggressive form of melanoma before summer arrived once more. Year after year, the deaths continued as if trying to keep up with the changing of the seasons. Fall, great-grandmother, old age. Winter, father-in-law, cancer. Spring, sixteen-year-old cousin, suicide. The cycle of death concluded with my mother, days after I turned forty.

Final tally: death—seven; years—five.

I spent the better part of those five years and then some at the bottom of a bottle trying to numb my pain. There hadn't been time to make my way through even a single stage of grief before another loss took center stage. Life wasn't supposed to be this way. I wasn't supposed to live in a constant state of mourning and sorrow, always wondering who'd be next. But this had become my reality. With each death, the heartache compounded. My world turned upside down, inside out, and backward. The titles which had defined me were gone. I was no longer Cal's granddaughter or Zack's sister. I would never again call anyone Mom or Dad. I didn't know how to deal with the overwhelming emotion or the loss of my identity. But I did know a few drinks at the end of the day would suspend reality for at least a few hours.

Just one more drink and I can forget about my grief.

Just one more and I can forget about my guilt.

Just one more and I can stop thinking about what I *should* have done.

Just one more and I can sleep tonight.

I had turned into a woman quick to anger and fearful every time the phone rang, wondering what bad news was coming next. I wanted to strangle every person who told me things would get better with time. Minor difficulties brought on bouts of sadness and despair. I felt like I had no one to talk to, or maybe, more accurately, that no one would understand.

I had always been the responsible one, the one whom friends and family, even my mother, would turn to for advice. I could think through problems in a logical manner, always able to suggest a solution, a way to work things out. But there was no way to work this out. There was only the downward spiral into blackness. I'd put on a pleasant face when I had to since constant sadness was a social faux pas, but the fact was I didn't want to share. I didn't want to talk about it. I only longed to escape.

I'd get up each morning and try to quell my hangover with coffee—at least enough to get my two boys, RJ and Tyler, out of bed and ready for the day, drop them at school, and go to work. But work was another source of feeling incompetent, I couldn't focus on anything other than the minutiae of a planned year-long adventure around the world—an adventure my husband and I had talked of often but which had faded into the background. The trip became a beacon in the darkness, a lighthouse shining the way home, a safe harbor out of grief's troubled waters. Rather than do my actual work of solving issues for clients, I'd sit at my desk, hiding behind my computer screen, and scour the Internet, site after site, searching for obscure places to visit, ignoring deadlines and clients' e-mails. I'd work on a budget for a year-long trip and investigate volunteer opportunities where my husband, Ray, a dentist, could provide services as we traveled. I examined how I could educate my two teen boys on the road. I was seeking the hidden corners of the world where grief couldn't find me. I was going through the motions of life, but in a cloud, only half present.

Ironically, right at the lowest point in my life, when I was begging for the universe to give me a break, it did just that. The details for the 'round-the-world trip we'd been dreaming about for years fell into place. We had done enough research to prepare our family for long-term travel; we had the means to make the trip a reality; all that was left was my willingness to let go of my fear and embrace the unknown. Easier said than done.

ESCAPE

Ray held the wine bottle up to the light to see how much was gone. "I think we need to reconsider the trip."

"What? Why?" I already knew why, but I wanted to hear him say the words out loud. I wanted him to put a voice to the thoughts swirling in my mind—you're a terrible mother, just as you were a disrespectful daughter; you're failing everyone; you're self-indulgent; you can't even get grief right.

Instead, Ray sat next to me on the couch and turned toward me. "I just don't think you're in a state to make the trip." He held my gaze for a moment, then dropped his head as if he'd just said the most painful words possible. Ray had no idea how much more destructive my own internal dialogue could be.

"Well, clearly I'm not right now." I hoped my words were not slurred. "The trip is still six months from now, Ray. I'll be fine."

"Lisa, maybe you should think about counseling."

This was not the first time he'd brought up counseling. Did I really need therapy? Probably. But all I could imagine was sitting in an office with an old guy in an argyle sweater and wire-rimmed glasses telling me to remember all my great memories, embrace the pain, remember you're not alone, *blah, blah, blah.*

Really? Get over it? Oh, okay, sure. Can you give me five easy steps?

I closed my eyes willing myself to stay calm. "Six months, Ray," I repeated, reaching for his hand. "I promise I'll get my shit together."

He wasn't done with me yet. "We can always postpone, go in a few years."

"No," I said, a little louder than I'd intended. "If we wait, the boys will be in high school and won't be able to go." I sighed and rubbed my head. "Honestly, I need to go. I feel like the trip is the only light I can see right now. We both know I'm not functioning very well here. I need a break from all this sadness."

Travis Air Force Base

Six months later, I sat with Ray and our two boys, RJ, fifteen, and Tyler, fourteen, in the modest passenger terminal of the Travis Air Force Base airport, midway between Sacramento and San Francisco, wondering if I was making a mistake. I looked around at the other passengers—some dressed in travel fatigues ready to embark on a new mission, others in civilian clothing with kids in tow ready for a family vacation. At first glance, the waiting area looked like any other terminal, except for a quiet that permeated the space. Though the floors were polished to a high shine and the rows of chairs were ordered to military precision, there was a heaviness to this space. This terminal had seen its fair share of grief, had greeted the families of fallen soldiers, served as a doorway for physically and mentally wounded troops, cradled friends and colleagues of survivors in the chairs now occupied by travelers. Though everyone around me was quiet, I felt alone in this understanding.

Ray was busy at his computer and the boys played on their gadgets. I struggled to focus long enough to remember what I was doing on my own computer. My thoughts vacillated between thinking a trip around the world was too big of an endeavor, and knowing I was desperate to escape the confines of my daily life that seemed to be always closing in on me. With a flight booked to Hawaii, I was now searching for a hotel room in Honolulu, but site after site showed little availability.

With more flights to Hawaii and Guam than any other military base on the west coast of the US, Travis Air Force Base was the first stop on our world tour. After a two-day, nine-hundred-mile drive to Travis from our hometown of Bellingham, Washington, my family of four had spent the better part of a week waiting for a flight heading west. Now confirmed on a flight to Hickam Air Force Base in Honolulu, we were headed in the right direction. But an hour of calls and scouring websites had not yielded a reasonably priced place to stay once we arrived—perhaps a minor setback for most people, but more than I could cope with.

"Did you try temporary family housing on base?" Ray asked.

"Yes," I answered, with a hint of annoyance.

"The Hale Koa on Waikiki?"

I tried to keep my voice down even though the words wanted to blast from my mouth. "Booked until Wednesday."

Of course I had tried all the military options. This was the problem with Space-A travel. Flexibility and adaptability are mandatory, and I was struggling with both. I looked around to make sure I hadn't drawn anyone else's attention. I had to imagine that at least some of these travelers were also facing the same problem. Why was I the only one who couldn't cope?

Everyone in the military can take advantage of the Space Available program, Space-A for short. As a dentist in the Public

Health Service, Ray was a member of the United States Uniformed Service, which allowed our family use of the program. Military planes fly from base to base all over the world every day, moving troops, equipment, and supplies. When there is extra space, the seats are offered to those traveling for personal reasons at little to no cost. The downside to Space-A is that flights are only posted seventy-two hours in advance and are often cancelled without notice or subject to change, sometimes mid-flight. I expected I'd have to scramble to find lodging and transportation as we moved from base to base. What I didn't expect was the escalation of my anxiety as we tried to pin down the details.

Sitting across the aisle, Ray stared at his laptop. "If you're having trouble, I can look."

"I'm not having trouble!" I snapped at him. "I know how to use a phone and a computer. I found a room, but it will cost us more than three hundred dollars a night, and who knows how long it'll be before the next hop."

This had been typical of our conversations lately. I'd take one word from Ray and read a whole book of judgment into it. Maybe he was trying to be helpful, but I couldn't see it. I only heard echoes of my incompetence.

Ray looked around at the other passengers in the terminal and then peered over his glasses, his hazel eyes locked on me as though trying to decide how to respond to my outburst. "We knew this part of the trip would be challenging. Just calm down. We'll figure it out." He looked back at his computer.

"You mean *I'll* figure it out. I don't see you helping. But maybe I'm just having *trouble*." I hated being told to calm down. My emotions boiling over, I opted for escape.

I made it to the bathroom as the tears spilled. I hated crying almost as much as being told to calm down, but lately it had become all too common an occurrence. I felt like I'd been knocked down and dragged through the dirt. The feelings of happiness and ease that had marked my early days of being a wife and mother had hardened almost to the point of inaccessibility. I'd started referring to this five-year period of loss as The Glitch. I needed to believe it was a finite period, a phase that was ending, an episode that could be contained and wrapped up neatly with a big black bow, that no one else I loved would join the ranks of the dead.

As I sat in the stall wiping the tears, I kept replaying the conversation with Ray. Why did I turn every conversation with him into a negative judgment? I didn't honestly believe he thought of me as incapable or stupid. The last thing I wanted was to push him away now, when we would need to rely on each other and be unified in our decisions.

I stepped out of the stall and made my way to the sink, running the water until it was ice cold. I didn't want my boys to see me crumbling for no apparent reason. When The Glitch began, RJ and Tyler were too young to have a solid understanding of death or the grief that comes along with it. But now, as teens, I knew they would be able to see I was suffering even if I didn't tell them directly.

I washed my hands and splashed my face, but avoided the mirror, knowing no amount of cold water would fade the dark circles under my eyes or bring life back to my colorless skin. I knew loss would be reflected in the down turned lines of my mouth, the dull-blue eyes staring back at me without their usual sparkle, the lax facial muscles that had forgotten how to smile.

At the last minute, I chanced a glance anyway.

This is why you need to go, Lisa. Jesus, look at yourself!

I was raised during a time when the media idealized the woman who could do it all—pilot a successful career, maintain a happy marriage, raise two gifted children, and still manage to cook, clean, head the PTA, and maintain a sexy physique. This had been my life, and I had flourished in the role of *super-woman* for a time. But The Glitch had cut my momentum off at the knees. For seven years, my ability to thrive as a wife and mother, let alone in my job as an IT consultant, waned with each death. All the life I had left, I poured into keeping up a "normal" appearance for my boys. Underneath the facade, however, weariness tempted me to drop into a soft bed and sleep until the world righted itself.

I patted my face and dried my hands, grimacing at the scratchy feel of the industrial paper towels on my skin. I took a deep breath and tried to relax my shoulders. I couldn't let my fears or the squabbling with Ray cloud the kickoff to the trip I'd dreamed of for most of my life. I didn't want my boys to sense my hesitancy and interpret it as fear. I didn't want to model surrender when life got too tough. This was my opportunity to leave my world behind, to discover new places where grief didn't linger, to figure out my new identity. I didn't want RJ and Tyler to live with a mom who was suffering all the time. I still wanted to be *superwoman*, or at least *supermom*, in their eyes. And even though it went against everything I'd ever heard about facing my problems head on, I knew the only way to get back to a place where equanimity was possible was to leave the world I knew behind.

I startled as the loudspeaker crackled to life. "Flight 89 to Hickam Air Force Base, Honolulu, Hawaii, will begin boarding in twenty minutes. Please have your boarding pass and identification ready." Time to get moving. I had to pull my shit together. I made sure the tears had been erased, straightened my clothes, and resolved to figure out lodging.

As I walked back to Ray and the boys, I caught sight of a faded poster on the wall showing a now pastel, once vibrant sunset at a secluded beach with a palm tree in the foreground, obviously a promotion for Hawaii. I recalled a friend saying, "If you get to Hawaii, look up Stacey. She just moved there with her husband." I had met Stacey only once before, years earlier, but I was willing to take a chance and contact her. She might have some insider tips on where to stay since she now called Hawaii home.

"I just remembered," I started before Ray could get in a word. I didn't want to launch back into a squabble. "I have an acquaintance in Hawaii I can check with to see if she has any ideas."

"Sure," he replied, no hint of agitation. "I'm looking, too."

I popped online, pulled up Facebook, and sent an instant message to Stacey detailing our dilemma, asking if she had any recommendations. Within minutes, my computer chimed as her response came in, "We have plenty of space for you all to stay here. Do you have a car, or do you need a ride?" Tears threatened again, but this time from relief.

"Guess what!?" I turned to Ray and the boys. "Stacey said we can stay with her."

"I told you things would work out. You really need to learn to use The Force." Ray shot me a playful grin.

Ray credited The Force for his calm and collected, everything-will-work-out-fine attitude. The same "these-are-not-the-droids-you-are-looking-for" Force from *Star Wars*. I first encountered his use of The Force on a trip to Florida when Ray wanted to visit his grandparents shortly after RJ was born.

Checking things off my planning list, I asked Ray, "Do you have their address?"

"Nope, we'll be fine. They haven't moved. I'm sure I can find it."

"When was the last time you were there?" I was concerned we'd end up driving in circles for hours in the Florida sun with an infant in the back seat.

"Maybe five years ago. Ten, possibly," he answered, still calm.

"Do you at least know what street it's on? I'm sure the town has grown. What if everything is different? Have you even told them we're coming?" The questions were pouring out as I thought of everything that could go wrong in our search for Grandma and Grandpa. "How do you expect to find their house?"

"I'll just use The Force," he said with complete seriousness.

Unconvinced, I printed out maps of the town and plotted out what we'd need to do when Ray's Force failed us. In the end, he drove right up to their place.

Looking at him now, I said, "I'm not sure The Force is enough to get us around the world."

"Well, it can't hurt. And you've done all the research you can possibly do. So, we're as prepared as we can be."

"I guess so," I mumbled.

In the months I'd spent researching long-term travel, I'd hoped to find tips and tricks, money-saving ideas and travel hacks, such as how to live out of a backpack for extended periods. I wanted to know how to find the best deals on hotels, the best places to take teens for education and wow factor, where to get local currency, and what to eat. I wanted some control over my environment by having as much planned as possible. But trying to define the minutiae only led to a heightened awareness that there was no way to have all the details figured out before we left, especially when we didn't know exactly where we were going.

Personal travel blogs had yielded a few interesting tidbits—like carrying a small bottle of peppermint essential oil to help with nausea, freshen your breath, relieve headaches when applied to your temples, help with odors, and even clear sinuses if dabbed under your nose. But through these blogs, I also uncovered a surplus of travel horror stories. I became acutely aware of the disastrous consequences when missing flights, running out of money, and getting sick. I had irrational fears about losing one of our kids, contracting a debilitating disease, or dying in a plane crash. And then there was finding lodging and food, getting our phones working in foreign countries, losing our belongings, having a bad time, kids fighting, parents fighting, doing a disservice to our kids by pulling them out of school for a year, carrying all my stuff in a backpack for months, or simply being American. These thoughts led to illogical fears about natural disasters, getting robbed, severe injury, terrorism, getting shot or kidnapped, and even being attacked by wild animals.

Before The Glitch I would have let these troubles fade into the background, staying aware of the possibilities but not letting the mere thought of disaster take the spotlight. Looking at my boys now, oblivious to the slew of potential calamities, I couldn't fathom how Ray remained so calm. I could only imagine this must be how agoraphobia starts.

"Mom, it's time to board. Let's go," Tyler called me to attention, his eyes alight with excitement, his hand extended to help me from my seat.

This was my moment to decide. As terrified as I was to take this journey, the thought of going back to a life filled with grief and self-doubt where I was struggling to function was far more terrifying. I watched Ray pack up his computer and help RJ gather his belongings. I took a last look around the crowded terminal, searching for my former self in the faces of strangers. I didn't see any sign of that vibrant young woman who'd been confident and ready to take on the world—no fear in her eyes, no hesitancy in her steps, no second thoughts as she picked up her backpack and walked with her husband and children onto the plane. I could see her clearly in the past, but I could no longer feel her presence. I could only hope that I might find her on this journey.

A HUI HOU
UNTIL WE MEET AGAIN

Honolulu, Hawaii

Stepping off the plane in Honolulu, a wave of heavy, humid air slammed into us. Temperatures soared, even by Hawaiian standards. We made our way via shuttle from Hickam Air Force Base to the Honolulu International Airport where Stacey was waiting. She sprang out of the car and hugged us as if we were long-missed relatives rather than mere acquaintances. I immediately felt comforted by her warm reception and couldn't help but think Ray might have something going with The Force.

She drove us to her home in Kaneohe, a single-story, white house that would have fit into any suburban neighborhood. Stacey showed us to our rooms and told us to make ourselves at home. As a bonus, we'd find her house had a pool, and she kept an "island car" (an extra vehicle for guests) and snorkeling gear at the ready for visitors. RJ and Tyler wasted no time finding their way to the backyard pool. Once settled, Ray and I sat with Stacey and chatted over cold beers, getting to know one another a little better. As the light faded and the air cooled, I called to the boys to get out of the pool and get ready for bed.

"Why do we have to go to bed so early?" Tyler asked. "I thought we were on vacation."

"Because we want to get started early tomorrow." I was still tense, not quite in vacation mode yet.

Technically, we were still in the United States and home was a short plane ride back to the mainland. We were simply in another location and, for me, the venue of my grief was still too close.

"Where are we going?" RJ asked, always wanting to know the plan.

"To the beach!" Ray answered with enthusiasm.

The next morning, we loaded up Stacey's island car with the snorkel gear and headed for Hanauma Bay. Once parked, we made our way to the entrance, where we paid to enter, and then watched a required nine-minute video to learn about the marine life, preservation, and conservation in the park. We exited the theater to a viewpoint overlooking the bay, below. The turquoise water was dotted with snorkelers in this once volcanic cone. We walked down a paved path, the sweet scent of plumeria mixing with sunscreen and salt water as we neared the beach. Finding a lovely shaded spot, we set out blankets and lathered up with sunscreen. Since we had only three sets of snorkel gear, I volunteered to sit out. I laughed as I watched Ray, RJ, and Tyler waddle to the water, stumbling along in their flippers.

Relaxed in the shade of the tall palms, I watched the sun dance over the waves, making the water sparkle. The sound of the waves crashing on the shore calmed me. Gulls wailing overhead and the din of others' conversations and children's laughter as they built sandcastles completed the picture of the perfect day on the beach. But even in this idyllic scene before me, all I could think about was the last time I was in Hawaii. My mother had guilted me into making the trip.

I remember Mom sitting at the kitchen table in her condo, rubbing her hands together for warmth against Washington's spring chill. "Why don't you take me to Hawaii before I die? You can do at least that much for me, can't you?" This talk about the end of her life, which doctors estimated around three to six months, was uncomfortable for both of us.

"I'm not sure it's practical, Mom." The truth was I didn't want to take the trip. In fact, I dreaded the thought of the whole escapade. Although my relationship with my mother had always been strained, the various chemical treatments, coupled with the radiation to slow the cancer spreading to her brain, had reduced her to a bitter, frail woman who thought she was invincible. She couldn't walk unassisted, relying on a cane in the house and a motorized wheelchair for anything outside. I had essentially taken over a life she could no longer manage—moving her into our home to care for her, paying bills, accompanying her to doctors' visits, keeping track of medications. How in the world did she think we could function in Hawaii?

"Oh, you think you know everything. I'll be fine. What, will I embarrass you? You're too good to travel with me?"

I tried to see the scared woman inside, fighting for her independence as long as possible, but her eyes communicated only disappointment in me. Did I owe her a dying wish?

Maybe I thought taking her somewhere would ease the harassment she so easily dished out to Ray and me, and even the boys. Maybe I was looking for a temporary escape from the suppressed grief that tagged along with me everywhere I went. Maybe I was giving in to her guilt trip about this being her dying wish—to spend time with me in Hawaii, one of her favorite places. Just the two of us.

I managed to get Mom to the island of Kauai, no small miracle considering she was struggling with stage IV cancer, dealing with open sores on her leg, unable to bend her knee, bald, moon-faced from high doses of cortisone, walking with a cane, and doped up on enough oxycodone to render an elephant unconscious.

We stayed in Kauai for five days, and every second was awful. Intoxicated and loopy from the medication, Mom refused sunscreen at the pool and invited strangers to our room to party, two of whom showed up one night to drink and chat her up until the wee hours of the morning. Later, she insisted we try zip-lining, scuba diving, and swimming with the dolphins.

"Mom, you have to be able to hike to go zip-lining," I tried to reason with her.

"You're so sure about everything, aren't you? Just call the damn number and find out. Maybe *they* will help a dying woman." She shoved a flyer for zip-line adventures across the table.

I dialed the number and spoke to the agent, asking about hiking distances and what kind of physical condition one would need to be in to zip line, the entire time looking directly at Mom and shaking my head.

"You are no fun at all. I'm going to the pool. Maybe I'll find some fun there!" She limped out of the room, cane in one hand, hanging on to walls with the other to steady herself.

I heard her shuffling around in her room, then leaving and slamming the door to emphasize her point. I put my head down on the table and exhaled all the air from my lungs. I only wanted to go back home, to be with Ray and the boys. This trip was turning out worse than I'd ever imagined. At sixty-one years old, Mom had turned into a mean, drunken adolescent with no intention of being corralled.

By the time I joined her at the pool, she'd talked scuba instructors into taking us diving the next day. She sat chatting to a young woman who was helping her fill out the questionnaire.

With pen and clipboard in hand, the instructor asked, "Are you currently taking medication that carries a warning about any impairment of your physical or mental abilities?"

Mom lied and said, "No."

"Mom—" I started, but she snapped her head in my direction, giving me a sidelong look that screamed: "if you open your mouth, I will never forgive you!" I was instantly reduced to my sixteen-year-old self, unable or unwilling to talk back and voice my objections.

"Don't worry, I'll pay for it," she said turning back to the instructor, as if money had been the cause of my hesitation.

How could the crew look at her bald head and gimpy, bandaged leg and think it a good idea to take her into the ocean?

In her excitement, Mom failed to ask about details, and we ended up on a dive starting from the shore, rather than a boat.

"Hold on to me!" she said as we entered the churning waters. Mom couldn't put her full weight on her cancerous leg and had to rely on me to support her.

We shuffled into the water, stepping over boulders, searching for steady footing, and bracing against the powerful waves, inch by inch. The instructor had marched past us with several other divers. I could see their heads bobbing up and down a few yards out. The impatient looks on their faces mirrored the thoughts in my head: What the hell was I doing out here with a woman who couldn't even stand on her own?

Once in the water, the instructor swam over to us and repeated the instructions on how to submerge. She then disappeared beneath the surface to join the others already several feet below us. I waited for Mom to submerge but she was unable to do anything besides float on the surface. I wasn't sure whether she couldn't follow instructions or hadn't been weighted properly. The instructor returned and repeated the instructions, but Mom wasn't listening.

She just kept dipping her face into the water, then lifting her head back up to shout, "Look at all the fish! What is the black-and-white one called?"

The instructor looked at me and tilted her head slightly as if to ask if everything was okay. I shook my head just enough for her to register that Mom was not fit for a diving expedition. The instructor went to relay to the other divers that the dive would need to be postponed until she could get us out of the water.

While we waited for the instructor's return, we floated at the surface, the waves continuing to toss us in every direction, causing us both to experience motion sickness and throw up. *Ahhh paradise*—bobbing up and down through your own vomit as fish swarm to gobble it up. In her drugged state, Mom didn't care if she was impeding the dive for others; I'm not even sure she registered the annoyance on their faces. She was thrilled by the number of fish the contents of our stomachs had attracted, and she chalked the day up as a success.

The only moments of peace I found in Hawaii were when I would sneak out in the early morning to walk alone on the beach or hike to tide pools and hidden waterfalls. The rest of the time, despite being surrounded by a lush, tropical paradise, I was miserable. I wanted to believe I had taken Mom to Hawaii to clear the air between us in preparation of her inevitable death, but that conversation would never happen. She was too far gone, too strung out from the medications, her brain too damaged by radiation. And I was too empty.

Ray shook his hair, sprinkling me with cool water. "Hey, Lis, ready to get in the water? The boys are waiting for you." He reached over me for a towel. "Are you okay?" His voice took on a softer quality.

I nodded and gave him a half smile. "I'm okay. Just remembering the last trip to Hawaii with Mom."

"Ah." I had told Ray all about the trip in my nightly calls home. "Well, go cool off and swim with the boys. RJ wants to show you the turtles." Ray was always pulling me back to the present, pointing me toward the two people who still brought joy to my life—my boys.

I put on the flippers and high-stepped my way to the water. I spotted the boys and waved.

RJ yelled, "Hurry, Mom."

Tyler pointed into the water and shouted, "The turtles are right here!" Then he submerged again.

I swam out to the boys and plunged my face into the ocean. Two sea turtles drifted in the current, oblivious to the swarm of gawking swimmers above. I let myself float on the surface, this time the waves were gentle. I looked at my boys and made a silent promise—I would never tear them down or treat them in a manner that would cause them to feel unworthy. I would always build them up and support them however I was able. Life, as I had learned, was far too short.

After our day of snorkeling, Stacey took us to dinner at a little hole-in-the-wall Mexican restaurant. Off a dark side street, miles from anywhere a tourist might wander, it met Ray's desire for the obscure. Inside this warehouse-turned-restaurant sat mismatched chairs surrounding eight-foot folding tables, lined up one after the other, cafeteria-style. After placing our orders at the counter near the door, we sat and poured ourselves drinks from the pre-mixed margarita bottle we brought along with us, BYOB being an accepted practice at locals-only establishments in Hawaii.

I took a big drink of the margarita, welcoming the familiar warmth coursing through my body, easing the tight grip emotion had bound up in every muscle.

As we sipped on cocktails, Stacey inquired about our plans. "Where do you think you'll go?"

"We're headed to Guam next to see my uncle and his family," I began. "After that, it's up in the air. We'll likely wind up somewhere with a military base—Tokyo, the Philippines, South Korea, Okinawa. After that, our only deadline is to get Ray to Da Nang, Vietnam, by October."

"I'm volunteering at a dental clinic for a month," Ray added.

"We actually have three volunteer sites set up for Ray," I said. "Vietnam in October, then Nepal in January, and Ghana in February."

"You don't seem super excited," Stacey said to me. "I think I'd be bouncing off the walls!"

Was she picking up on my anxiety? "I worry a lot about this being the right decision."

"The right decision for who? It's obviously the right decision for you all. What are you worried about?"

"I worry about everything," I said. I rolled my eyes trying to demonstrate a sense of humorous exasperation at my own unease. I didn't want to let on just how anxious I really was. "I tend to focus on all the things that could go wrong."

What I couldn't say out loud was that I was terrified of losing one of my boys or Ray. Although it had been two years since the last casualty of The Glitch, I had yet to be convinced that death would not sneak up and steal another loved one.

"But what if the opposite is true? Think of all the things you'll see and experience together—just the four of you." Stacey's voice rose an octave exhibiting the fire of her enthusiasm. "How many people can say they have traveled around the world? Not many that I know. And with your boys in tow? C'mon! That's an incredible journey that could shape you in ways you never imagined. And if you have bumps along the way," she leaned back in her chair and laughed, "well, don't misadventures make the best stories, anyway?"

The gleam in Stacey's eyes and excitement in her voice were more than the margarita talking. She said all the things I'd imagined when we dreamed up this trip. Of course, she would see only the excitement of the journey. She didn't know me, didn't know the toll The Glitch had taken on my confidence. All she knew was that my family was setting out on a grand adventure and that I was a worrier. That's all I'd let her see.

But Stacey knew the joy and wonder that could be experienced when you let go of all the things holding you back. She had given up her life on the mainland and followed her heart's desire to Hawaii. Her enthusiasm was contagious.

Our meals arrived and we all reached for forks to dig in. "Ready for another?" Stacey asked, bottle ready to pour over my glass.

I covered my glass with my hand. "No, I'm good."

After only three days in Hawaii, a flight to Guam popped up, and it was time to say goodbye. Stacey insisted on driving us to the airport to see us off. Promises to "keep in touch" and "visit again" accompanied hearty hugs.

We stepped onto the sidewalk and Stacey gave us a last "a hui hou," and a wave goodbye.

As we entered the terminal, I marveled at this woman who had welcomed four near-strangers into her home and treated them like family. Her enthusiasm for adventure radiated through her every word, and I was sad to leave. I closed my eyes and replayed her words in my mind: "You will treasure this adventure for the rest of your lives." Until we meet again, indeed.

"Well, that worked out really well, didn't it," Ray said, giving my arm a nudge.

"Yep, I'm sure glad I remembered the advice to call Stacey," I replied with a smile, returning the nudge.

"I'm thinking The Force might have played a little part in it," he teased.

"Whatever."

But it did seem when I let go of my worries, even for a moment, the stars aligned and we had a place to stay, a car, and a new friend in Hawaii. Was the universe trying to tell me to relax and let go? Embrace the unknown and move forward on the journey? Of course, maybe that's just what The Force is— the metaphysical power of the universe, an energy created by all living things, a light in the darkness. I wanted to believe in some kind of collective energy providing me with what I needed at just the right time. I just wasn't sure I was ready to call it *The Force*.

Days of Travel: 10
Miles Logged: 3,391

MIRROR MIRROR

Guam

Our flight from Hawaii to Guam was a chilly but uneventful eight-hour flight. The military cargo plane offered little in terms of comfort. Lacking the internal structure of overhead bins, cushioned seating, and paneling, the shell did little to keep heat in or noise out. Cargo nets ran lengthwise down each side of the bare metal interior, individual seats denoted only by seatbelts at regular intervals. Ear plugs or earphones had to be worn at all times and, once at cruising altitude, layers were a must. The upside to traveling on a military cargo plane was that we were not subject to the same rules and regulations as commercial flights. We could get up and walk around without fear of getting blocked from our seat by the beverage cart. The downside—there was no beverage cart. Should we get tired, we could roll out a mat or sleeping bag and lie down in front of the cargo nets and sleep, provided we had brought our own sleeping bag or mat.

"Where's your sweatshirt, RJ?" I asked before the plane took off, hoping he had it tucked away where I couldn't see it.

"It'll be hot in Guam," he said, not answering my question.

Getting RJ to put on a sweatshirt was like trying to put a collar on a feral cat. Getting him to answer a direct question wasn't much easier. RJ was always trying to move one step beyond the immediate conversation.

"Yes, but it will be cold for eight hours while we're flying over the ocean," I reminded him.

"Grandma was there before, right?" asked Tyler, saving RJ from my sweatshirt interrogation.

"Grandma was there a couple times," I said to the boys as I dug through my pack. "Do you remember the pictures of your Uncle Zack jumping into the pool?"

Mom had been to Guam twice to visit her brother, John—the last time with my brother when he was in high school. She'd brought Zack there intending to leave him with John. She imagined a life away from his peers and the bad habits he'd adopted could be replaced with white sandy beaches and warm, tropical sun. Ultimately, she couldn't bear to return to the States without him.

"It'll be so nice to get off this cold plane and relax in the sunshine this afternoon." Ray clasped his hands behind his head and leaned back, basking in the imagined warmth of the sun. "We can take a nice swim in the pool and work on our tans."

"Put in your earplugs," I reminded everyone. "Let's try to get some rest. Our time zones will be all messed up when we get to Guam." We'd barely had enough time in Hawaii to get used to the three-hour time difference, and now we'd be adding another four-hour change and flip-flopping night and day.

Our main reason for visiting Guam was to see my mom's youngest brother, Uncle John, along with his wife Lucy, and their fifteen-year-old daughter, Jaden. It didn't hurt that Guam had two busy military bases with weekly flights and happened to be on our path toward Asia.

I'd last seen John at my brother Zack's funeral seven years earlier, but I hadn't seen Aunt Lucy or Jaden in more than a decade. While I was excited to visit my family on this faraway tropical island, I didn't want to be asked the inevitable question, "How are you doing?" As soon as those words rolled off the tongue, I'd have to decide to either be honest and admit I was far from okay, or I'd have to lie. The truth is hard. It invites others into the blackness of my soul. I didn't want to chat about the worst years of my life. The simple courtesy of asking how I was doing had become a reminder of everything I'd lost. In my experience, most people didn't want to hear I was struggling to stay upright, struggling daily not to keep reliving in my mind what I'd been through, wondering what I could have done differently. That an emotionally numb, alcohol-fueled version of the girl I used to be had taken my place. They'd rather hear I was okay, that I was at least making my way through the grief process. In Guam, I knew I would not be the only one to have experienced loss during The Glitch. John also lost his father, sister, and nephew. My standard response of "fine" would not suffice for people who not only knew my story but were characters in the same book.

Each donning a heavy sweatshirt and earplugs, we arranged ourselves on the bare metal floor and tried to settle in. We traveled light, each taking only a single backpack and smaller day pack. The beginning of our journey would be primarily in sweltering Asian countries. Heavy sweatshirts and long pants would have added unneeded weight to our packs. The biggest thing weighing me down at this point was the plastic bag containing Mom's ashes I was lugging around in my travel purse.

Mom had not given me a directive on what to do with her ashes once she was gone, but she had purchased a shiny decorative box for her remains, presumably to be kept somewhere in my house, though she never said as much. We kept the box on the bookshelf in our living room for a few months, but jokes about her listening in on conversations and watching over us made everyone in the house uncomfortable. Eventually, she was relegated to a back bedroom until we figured out what to do with her. I didn't want to spread her ashes just anywhere. I still had some longing for closure, as if giving her a grand send-off might unburden my heavy heart.

When the trip became a reality, I had asked John what he thought about spreading her ashes in Guam, since he hadn't come back to the States for her funeral. He agreed Guam would be a suitable resting place. I removed the sealed bag of ashes from the lacquered box and crammed the ten-pound bag in the only free space I had left—my purse. At least the bag of ashes could serve as a travel pillow for this leg of the journey.

RJ snuggled up next to me. "Is this the same plane Grandpa Cal flew?" he asked, studying the interior of the plane.

"Not exactly, but it's similar," I said. "I don't think the plane he flew is still in service. This is probably a newer version."

"Does John fly planes like Grandpa Cal?" Military planes fascinated RJ.

"I don't know what he does, but we can ask. Get some rest," I answered, hoping to end the questions.

I pulled RJ in close, hoping to give each of us an added boost of warmth. I wondered what state I would find John in. How had the loss of his sister, his lifelong confidante, affected him? Did he wish, like me, that he had done more to help Zack?

As the first American territory touched by the sun's early morning rays, Guam's motto is "Where America's Day Begins." Located in Micronesia, just west of the International Dateline, Guam is closer to China, Japan, and Australia than it is to the United States. It is not a typical destination for American tourists but is inhabited by several thousand Americans due to its strategic military location. This tiny island, five times smaller than Rhode Island, is home to both a US Naval base on the southwest side of the island and a US Air Force base on the northeast side.

After landing, I phoned John to let him know we'd arrived. Half an hour later, he drove up in an old, extended cab pickup truck dented and scraped from years of abuse, paint peeling from exposure to the salt and sand. As he exited the cab, I noticed John, not yet sixty, looked more like seventy. He appeared more worn out since I'd seen him last. He had gained weight, and his once salt-and-pepper hair, peeking out from an ancient baseball cap, had turned almost entirely gray. His tanned skin did little to hide the deep wrinkles in the folds of his neck and the crow's feet stretching out from both eyes. I marveled at the family resemblance I'd never noticed before, and how much he reminded me of my mom and grandpa.

"*Hafa Adai*, Lisa girl!" John boomed when he saw me, a smile in his voice, but not on his lips. *Hafa Adai*, pronounced "half-a-day," means "hello" in Chamorro, an Austronesian language of the indigenous people of Guam.

"I've been waiting for you guys for days." John shuffled toward us in broken-down flip-flops. "What took you so long to get here?"

"Oh, you know military flights. Not quite as scheduled as commercial flights," I answered, as he wrapped me in a tight bear hug.

The question was rhetorical. John knew all about the unpredictability of Space-A flights, having served in the Air Force for over twenty years, and still employed by the USAF in a civilian capacity. At least he didn't ask how I was doing.

"Well, I'm glad you finally made it." John hugged me again. I wondered if he was assessing the toll on my physical appearance the same way I was assessing his.

"Nice to see you again, Ray." John greeted Ray with an equally exuberant hug.

Then, John looked the boys up and down. "Man, you boys have gotten big! What's she feeding you guys?"

"Lots of vegetables," Tyler said with a grin.

We each picked up a backpack and loaded into the truck. John pulled his cap low on his brow, shielding his eyes from the morning sun. As we drove, he gave us a running commentary about the many buildings on the base, filling up our tired silence with information that would be useless to us, but served to avoid anything deeper.

Andersen Air Force Base felt distinctly American with tidy, paved roads and neutral, square buildings, surrounded by cut grass and pruned trees. As we exited the gates, however, we left the manicured space and were at once engulfed by jungle. With a constant tropical climate, the lush vegetation would swallow everything if not tamed daily. Even more than Hawaii, Guam felt like a jungle. And at only thirteen degrees north of the equator, the temperature was a predictable eighty-five almost every day of the year, with humidity hovering around ninety percent. Emerging from the jungle, the villages in Guam could have been any other small town back on the US mainland, except for the signs with lettering in Japanese or Chamorro.

Pulling up to the house, I noted the exterior was in as much disrepair as John and his truck. The sun had taken its toll on the paint, now dull and faded. Shutters meant to block the sun and wind were missing slats and some shutters were missing entirely. Was this the same house we'd seen in pictures from Mom and Zack's visit? I glanced at Ray and the boys, but no one else seemed to take any notice of the dilapidation. Maybe they didn't understand how John's appearance, his truck, the run-down house were all reflections of his grief, but I could see surrender in every dent and scratch, every peeling paint chip and broken shutter. I guessed surviving the day until he could crack open a beer probably took every ounce of energy he had. I looked at the house and then at John. My heart ached for him. I knew I was not alone in my struggle. I'd been trying to leave the grief behind, but here it was, mirrored right back at me.

The sun was steadily rising, and we were all feeling the effects of the tropical heat and hours of restless overnight travel.

"I'll let you guys get settled and then we can go explore," John said as he parked the truck.

"Do we have time for a quick dip in the pool before we go?" I asked, desperate for a little relief from the heat and emotion that threatened to surface.

"We have time, but the pool is empty." John rubbed his forehead, then pulled the brim of his cap back down on his head.

I felt the collective deflation from Ray and the boys and hoped John couldn't feel it too.

John shook his head, looking overwhelmed. "Has a crack somewhere. I haven't gotten out to fix it yet. C'mon in, it's cooler in here," he added, opening the door to his home.

Inside, everything was neat and intact, a complete contrast to the exterior, almost museum-like. The living room contained intricately carved wooden sculptures and exquisite works of native Chamorro art depicting ancient island life. Tables and shelves shone with fresh furniture polish. The space was tidy, not a single decoration askew.

"This is really beautiful," I said.

John shrugged. "Yeah, it's Lucy's doing. Nice to look at, but not very functional."

Actually, this seemed more functional than a dilapidated truck and cracked pool, but I didn't say as much. Upkeep on this pristine space had to be Lucy's way of keeping her life intact in any area she could as she watched John deteriorate. She, like Ray, probably didn't know what else to do. Lucy had to keep one area of her life unblemished, as grief decayed her home and her husband.

I looked at my family. I knew I'd been neglectful. Maybe it hadn't reached the same level as John's neglect of his person and property, but I was on the same continuum. Although all my relationships had suffered as I trudged from one loss to the next, my relationship with Ray had fared the worst. Grief had become demanding and all-consuming. I struggled to stay upright, faltering as I tried to keep up with the world continuing to spin around me. It took all my energy just to get through each day. I had nothing left for him. But he stood by me, nonetheless, compensating for my withdrawal. He was my safety net, for better or worse, the one who was holding me up when I couldn't stand on my own. I longed to be whole again.

John showed us around the house and then to our rooms. "I'm going out for a smoke. Let me know when you're ready to tour the island."

"Great." I knew I was about to hear from everyone how *not* great things were. "We'll just get changed and then we'll be ready."

As soon as we heard the sliding glass door to the porch close, I said what I could tell was on everyone's mind. "Well, that stinks. I was really hoping for a pool. Let's at least get out of these warm clothes and then go see the island."

RJ and Tyler agreed and went to change.

I wiped away the sweat collecting on my forehead and peeled off my long pants and shirt that sweat had glued to my body. Even shorts and a tank top didn't help me feel any cooler. I'd been so looking forward to a refreshing swim in the pool. Instead, I lay on the bed under a blanket of oppressive air and permeating sadness, the ceiling fan doing nothing to diminish either.

"Okay, Mom, we're ready to go," said Tyler. He and RJ had changed into shorts and T-shirts.

I sat up from the bed, knowing I had to rally all the energy I had left.

"Let's go find John," I said.

We found him sitting out back in a weather-worn chair straining under his weight. The porch was strewn with old pots and planters, many containing dead and desiccated plants. The pool sat empty, filled with debris. An enormous palm tree, its trunk at least two feet in diameter, lay uprooted across part of the overgrown lawn.

"Wow, what happened to the tree?" I asked.

"Lost it in the last typhoon," John replied.

"When did that happen?" Had we arrived during typhoon season?

"Ah, I don't know, maybe a couple years ago." The tree was more evidence of John's debilitation and suggested it was not a recent decline. "Y'all ready to see Guam?" he asked.

"Sure. Let's go."

"Bring your swimsuits. There's a swimming hole a few miles down the road."

Had John caught sight of our disappointment? Maybe the sight of us all dripping sweat had planted the idea.

The kids cheered. That we might actually get to swim after all perked up everyone's spirits—even mine.

After meandering south on the two-lane road that runs around the island, we came to the town of Inarajan, considered the oldest village in Guam. Just off the road, a natural saltwater lagoon, protected from the waves by a sand and coral barrier, beckoned. Here, ocean waves could reach at least six-feet high as they approached land, but the pool saw only minor ripples due to the protective reef.

RJ and Tyler didn't hesitate to jump right in, especially after they found the water was eighty degrees. I sat on a rock at the edge of the pool and dangled my feet in the water while Ray and John caught up on all the sports happenings on the mainland. Watching the boys splash and tag each other, I was reminded of the summer after my high school graduation, when Mom moved my brother and me from Butte, Montana, to Bellingham, Washington. While neither of us was overjoyed about the move, Zack and I were thrilled to find that our condo had a pool.

While Mom worked, Zack, then five, and I, seventeen, spent sunny days by the pool, just the two of us. I taught him to swim that summer. I could still picture his wide smile and feel his delight as he made his way across the pool for the first time on his own.

"I did it, Sissy!" He shook the water from his short blond hair.

"Great job, bud! I knew you could do it."

As I sat with my bare feet dangling in the warm water, I imagined even now how it could have been me and Zack splashing around. I wished I could go back and force my mother to

see what was happening with Zack as he became a teen, clue her into the fact that he was screaming for help.

Even though Guam would be considered a small island, only thirty-miles long by nine-miles wide, there were a multitude of hidden beaches, Spanish and WWII monuments, and swimming holes to explore. Our days fell into a predictable pattern. We'd rise early to have breakfast with Lucy, sharply dressed in a pressed suit, and Jaden, equally smart in her starched Catholic school uniform, before sending them off to work and school. When John had enough coffee to clear the remaining cobwebs from the previous day's consumption, we'd set off for a new part of the island to explore. On the road by 9:00 a.m., John would stop at an historical marker or other significant landmark, and then hit a roadside mart by 11:00 a.m. to buy beer. With one beer downed and another cracked open in the cup holder, John would continue driving to the next location. Glancing at Ray and the boys, I could see the looks of concern in each of their faces. I was thankful the speed limit in Guam never topped thirty-five miles per hour.

Upon our return to the house each day, John would stake out a seat at the kitchen table, pop open another beer, and take regular trips to the back porch to smoke until Lucy and Jaden returned home for the evening. Over dinner and into the night, we talked about our travel plans, reminisced about happy parts of the past, and shared the three teens' plans for the future. I watched my uncle quench the demons rattling around in his head, his mood going up as each beer went down, I recognized in him a grown man who'd been emotionally abandoned by his parents, suppressing the difficult emotions with alcohol. He may have been present physically, but emotionally he was void. Even sequestered on this island, he couldn't escape the past. My mother was a product of the same parents and her subsequent parenting had left me emotionally unattended, too. Sitting at the dinner table, I acknowledged to myself with a heavy heart that I was on the path toward repeating the same pattern with my children, choosing to withdraw and suppress my emotions rather than be fully engaged with them. I wondered if this is what Ray saw when he looked at me.

After dinner one night, RJ and Tyler joined Jaden for a movie, John retired to the back porch with beer and cigarettes at the ready, while Lucy busied herself with cleaning up.

"Can I do anything to help?" I asked.

"No, no, I've got this. Why don't you and Ray take a stroll around now that it's not so hot outside," Lucy suggested.

I looked at Ray. "Wanna go for a walk?"

Because Guam was near the equator, there were exactly twelve hours of light and twelve hours of dark every day. By 7:00 p.m., it was pitch-black outside. Ray and I strolled through the neighborhood enjoying the quiet. I needed the walk more than I realized.

As we approached the end of a road, Ray asked, "Is everything okay? You're awfully quiet."

I let out a deep sigh. "I didn't expect to have Mom and Zack so much on my mind while I was here. I can't help but wonder if both might still be alive if she'd left him here with John."

Mom had married for the third time when I was hitting the awkward preteen stage of twelve, the perfect age for a built-in babysitter. When my brother was born, I became a mini mommy. I loved rocking him to sleep and playing with him. But when Mom and her husband divorced two years later, playing mommy became all too real. I was tasked with babysitting Zack every day. From the time I was out of school until whenever Mom came home—sometimes five o'clock in the evening and sometimes midnight—Zack was in my charge.

I'd take him everywhere with me, out to the local video arcade where I'd dole out quarters for games while I gossiped with friends, to the swimming pool where he'd cling to me and splash in the shallow water. Friends knew if they asked me to go anywhere, chances are I'd have Zack with me, this little towheaded boy with big brown eyes who'd hold my hand and tell us silly jokes. Adults remarked about how mature I was and how much responsibility I could handle. Taking charge and getting things done became expected traits.

At seventeen, as I prepared to graduate from high school, I talked increasingly about leaving home. In response, Mom clung to Zack as if he were the only person in the world who loved her. Perhaps needing to make a move before I did, seven days after graduation, Mom took a job out of state, packed up the house, and moved us all to Bellingham. But it quickly became clear our living situation was not working.

As I sipped coffee one morning, doing my best to wake up, Zack wandered into the living room and said, "Good morning, Sissy."

Not quite at full attention, I gave him a wink and croaked out "Hi, bud" in a whisper.

Mom didn't hear my hushed response and stormed into the living room. Zack stood wide-eyed, not comprehending why Mom was so upset. She demanded to know why I hadn't responded to him.

I rolled my eyes, set my jaw. "I did respond."

I did not hide my revulsion for her. She must have sensed how much I wished to get away from her, might have intuited the schemes I was concocting in my head to escape the responsibility of taking care of them both.

Looking for an ally, she turned to Zack and demanded, "Did she say good morning to you?"

Afraid of giving the wrong answer, Zack looked up at her and said, "No."

He was correct. I hadn't said good morning, strictly speaking.

She turned and pointed at me. "If you think you're too good for us, what are you still doing here?"

I looked at Zack, his innocent gaze begging me to tell him what was happening. I knew I had to leave, that Zack would stand a better chance at normalcy without me. If I stayed, she would continue to drive a wedge between us, pulling Zack close and continuing to push me away. Before the day was over, I had packed my bags and moved out for good. Terrified, but not seeing any other options, I went back to Montana. I enrolled in college at seventeen, worked seven part-time jobs to make ends meet—everything from theater usher to babysitting, calling keno to legal assistant—and took on all the responsibilities and demands of living on my own. I didn't always enjoy my rush from school to jobs, but I did what I had to do to survive.

Within a few months of my departure, Mom and I resumed speaking to each other, never resolving the issues of the past, but at least moving forward. When the stresses of school and work became too much for me to handle, I quit college and moved back to Bellingham. In the three years I had been absent, things had changed drastically. I was shocked at the relationship between Mom and Zack. She let my brother, then only eight years old, get away with everything—staying up too late, skipping homework, hanging out with friends who, even in grade school terms, seemed like trouble. There was little positive discipline, no consequences for any of his actions. Zack sought acceptance and guidance outside her rule and fell in with a rough crowd. Even though I was only a young woman, instinctively I knew my mother was making poor choices and failing to take a hard line with Zack when he needed it. Any attempt to broach the subject of parenting or discipline with her was met with an icy stare and a tight mouth.

By age twenty-six, I had moved into a life of my own, working crazy hours during the dot-com boom, building a relationship with Ray, and starting a family. I watched from a distance as Zack pulled further and further away from Mom as he entered his teens, while she tumbled deeper and deeper into depression.

"I don't know what to do. He's hanging with some rough people," Mom said to me one day over coffee after Ray and I had been married for a couple of years. "Sometimes he comes home and goes straight to bed. I think he might be drinking or doing drugs."

"Mom, he's begging for your attention. He wants you to step in," I said.

Somewhere in the back of her mind she had to know this. I imagined some separation where Zack could get counseling would benefit them both, and I'd found several wilderness camps and rehabilitation facilities where he could go, but Mom resisted.

"He'll barely talk to me now. If I send him to one of those camps, he'll never talk to me again."

"He might not talk to you for a while, but he won't be doing drugs or hanging out with the wrong crowd! It'll give you both time to get some help." I knew my words were having no effect. Mom didn't want to hear that she was part of the problem.

She stared down at her hands. "He'll never come back."

Before his senior year of high school, when Zack's behavior deteriorated and his drug use increased, Mom had taken him to

Guam, intending to leave him there with John. Her hope was for Zack to finish school and find an active job on the water, leading dives or jet-ski tours. But Mom and Zack ended up having a fantastic time together and by the time the trip was over, she couldn't bear to go back home without him.

So, Zack flitted back and forth between his dad's house in Montana and Mom's house in Washington, leaving one place for the next when trouble caught up with him. When Zack's drug addiction escalated to a point where it could no longer be ignored, Mom staged an intervention.

During the initial meeting, before confronting Zack, the interventionist laid his hand gently on Mom's shoulder and asked, "Do you have a recovery home picked out for him?"

She wiped away tears and nodded. "Yes, there's a place outside Missoula I've made arrangements with."

"Missoula?" I interrupted. "Mom, he'll be out of there in a day. All he has to do is call up a friend to come and get him! Do you understand how serious this is?" I was furious with her for being so shortsighted.

"I have to agree with your daughter." His voice was calm as he addressed my mother. "I can arrange for him to attend a program in Florida. It will be much harder to drift back into old patterns if he's outside his home base," the interventionist added.

Against my protestations and the advice of the interventionist, Mom sent him to the recovery house in Montana. He lasted only three days before making that call and turning right back to the needle to find his own escape. He moved in with some friends and didn't speak to either of us for months.

Zack was just twenty-three to my thirty-five when I returned to Butte for my dad's funeral, the first of The Glitch. Zack stayed by my side the entire weekend, helping me deal with the death of my father. Not quite fifty-nine, my dad had died of a massive heart attack brought on by years of hard drug use.

I hugged Zack and then held him at arm's length. "Look at me." When I was sure he really saw me, I continued. "I'll do everything in my power to help you succeed, but nothing to help you fail."

Zack promised he was sober and making progress at his warehouse job in Moses Lake, a small town of twenty thousand in central Washington. We spoke often after my dad's funeral and I could tell by his clear tone and sense of pride he was genuinely working on his recovery. But in the end, it wasn't enough.

After a painful dentist appointment, Zack was tempted into taking a dose of methadone. That one dose proved to be too much for his abused body. In the middle of the night, as Zack lay sleeping, his heart slowed and his breathing faltered until both stopped completely. When his girlfriend tried to wake him for work the next morning, she found him dead.

I didn't tell a soul I had spoken to Zack the night he died, perhaps while the drugs were racing through his system already slowing his heart and respiration. I didn't tell anyone I'd made empty promises about getting together with Zack, knowing full well I had no intention of having my kids around him until I knew for sure he was clean. Throughout his funeral and the events that followed, I just sat with that memory. I wondered if I could have said something different in my last conversation with Zack, but I knew his path was set in motion years before that phone call. The truth was that I blamed only one person for my brother's untimely death—my mother.

With Lucy and Jaden home from work and school for the weekend, the mood in the house lifted. Even John's mood improved. Perhaps Lucy and Jaden were the lights in his darkness.

Early one Saturday morning, Ray and I slipped away with the boys and Jaden to go snorkeling. We drove to the southwest corner of the island where the waves were calm. We planned to swim out to a shallow sand bar and reef a hundred yards offshore. While Ray explored the tide pools with Tyler and RJ, Jaden and I donned our fins and masks and started the swim. Colorful fish flitted this way and that before our faces. Calm washed over me until I began to lose sight of the ocean floor. The water became a deep, hazy blue in every direction and as dark as midnight below me. The schools of fish darting in every direction had disappeared. Jaden and I were alone, swimming in a blue void.

With my mouth plugged by the breathing tube and my ears submerged, the only thing I could hear was my breath moving in and out, which suddenly sounded exceptionally loud. Unable to see beyond the edge of my goggles, I often lost sight of Jaden and stopped to look for the spout of her snorkel poking out of the water. Once confident I was heading in the right direction and still had a companion, I put my face back in the water and resumed swimming, the theme music from *Jaws* alternated with Dory's voice in *Finding Nemo* singing, "Just keep swimming. Just keep swimming. Just keep swimming, swimming, swimming."

The hundred yards we estimated felt more like a mile. I was relieved when the deep blue lightened as the ocean floor rose and the sand bar came into view. Jaden and I planted our fins carefully among the coral, happy to have made it across the open stretch. Once I caught my breath, I held the mask up to my eyes and dipped my face in the water to watch blue sea stars, giant hermit crabs, and schools of colorful fish darting all around the coral and rocks.

"That was quite a swim," I said to Jaden. "It was farther than I thought."

"I know, right? But I'm glad we did it. I haven't ever been out here," she replied.

"Really? Why not?" I asked, before I could stop myself. I could guess the answer.

"We don't really do much snorkeling anymore."

"Well, I'm happy to be out here with you."

Jaden smiled. "Me too."

I looked all around, stunned by the beauty of my surroundings. I studied the vibrancy of the glowing water in every direction and the fish darting around my legs. I memorized the feeling of the sun on my skin and the smell of the ocean. This was a moment I wanted to remember forever.

When I shielded my eyes and looked across the open expanse in search of Ray and the boys, I felt as far away from them emotionally as I was physically, an expanse between us. But I could see all I had to do was swim back to them.

After our snorkeling adventure, we returned to the house to find John at the kitchen table tipping back a cold beer.

"Do you want to talk about what to do with Mom's ashes?" I asked, biting my lip. I hoped John and Lucy weren't as reluctant to talk about it as I seemed to be.

"We've been talking about it." John nodded toward Lucy, who was busy tidying up the house. "Lucy, what'd we decide? Jinapsan?"

"Lou loved it there, that would be a great place! We'll make a day of it," Lucy answered, with more enthusiasm than I expected. I'd always loved how Lucy called my mom "Lou," a shortened version of her middle name, Louise.

"What is Jinapsan?" I asked.

"It's a beach up by Anderson and the Ritidian Beach refuge. It's privately owned, but currently landlocked," John explained, as he rubbed the ache out of his hands. "The only way to get to the beach is to go onto the base and then drive over the sand when the tide is low. It'll be quiet up there."

"Your mom loved going there. It'll be a great place to send her off on the outgoing tide," Lucy said.

I had to agree. Mom loved tropical beaches and adventure. I attributed some of my wanderlust to her. Even though we rarely ventured far from Montana when I was a child, Mom always had dreams of seeing the world. We'd watch movies about far-away places and talk about everywhere we'd go if she ever won the lottery or struck it rich.

When Ray and I really dug into our world trip planning, Mom was two years into her battle with cancer. As Ray and I discussed cities and countries we wanted to see, she'd often interrupt.

"Will you wait until I'm gone to leave?" she'd ask.

I could feel her eyes watching me, studying me for clues as if she were a detective trained in detecting lies by facial features alone. Her words were pushing me into a corner from which there was no escape.

"Mom, you're not going to die anytime soon."

I didn't know at the time how wrong that statement was. I believed her treatment would be successful, and she'd find a desire to live again. At least I hoped she'd find something to live for other than me.

When Zack died, Mom focused her clinginess on me. Her depression worsened and she let her own friendships lapse. She inserted herself into my circles. If I had friends over for dinner or a game night without inviting her, she'd sequester herself for days, then lecture me on my insensitivity. I began to tiptoe around her, afraid any wrong move would set her off.

So, when she asked, "What if I die while you're away? Will you come home?" I could only answer by deflecting.

"I don't know. What kind of question is that?" I answered, with a sinking feeling in my stomach. I knew the real answer was "No."

"There are so many places I wanted to see and now I'll never have that chance. Will you take my ashes and spread a bit in each country you visit?" she asked with a little spark of hope.

I agreed to take her ashes just to get off the topic, but I knew there was no way in hell I would carry them all around the world and sprinkle a little here and there. That would be like reliving her manipulation, day after day. In her final days, nothing less than my full attention would suffice. It seemed nothing short of putting my life on hold—spending every waking moment with her, abandoning my family obligations while I waited for her to die—would satisfy her. But I couldn't simply put my own family aside for an undetermined length of time. My emotions tore me in two. I felt forced to choose between her and my husband and children.

The tug-of-war on my responsibilities ended when cancer declared victory, and my mother died. But I still carried the burden of guilt and trying to do right by my mother. Here I was, five thousand miles from home, lugging her ashes around in my purse. I'd considered "forgetting" her ashes at home or simply throwing them out with the trash. Who would know? *I bet that's a part of the world you never thought you'd see.* But my fantasies of revenge were short-lived. I couldn't just throw her away. For all the anger and resentment we'd endured from each other in the last years of her life, she was still my mother.

On a bluebird sky, tropical Sunday morning, we packed up picnic supplies and headed for Jinapsan Beach. I've often heard people say Hawaii is a tropical paradise unequaled in beauty. They are wrong. Guam takes all the good parts of Hawaii and multiplies them tenfold. As we wound our way onto the sand and around giant boulders, the deserted white sandy beach opened before us, bordered by lush green jungles sprawling down cliffs on one side, and by crystal-clear, turquoise waters on the other.

After setting out our chairs and blankets, exploring the area, and taking a cool swim in the ocean, we decided it was time to let Mom go. I stood knee-deep in the waves, John, Lucy, and Jaden to my right, Ray, RJ, and Tyler to my left, everyone close enough to touch, but none of us doing so. I opened the sealed bag and poured the ashes into the water. A bright white cloud formed and lapped at our legs as we all stood mesmerized by the unexpected beauty of ashes mixing with the sea.

"Should we say something?" Ray asked.

Lucy looked to me, but I was at a loss for words. "We love you, Lou!" she yelled, her words echoing off the nearby cliffs.

"Happy travels," I added, imagining Mom finally getting her wish to see the world.

The cloud of ashes in the shallow ocean water continued to hover around our feet as if reluctant to leave before dissipating little by little and washing farther out into the sea.

Days of Travel: 27
Miles Logged: 7,341

I M NOT THAT GIRL

Okinawa, Japan

After nineteen days, we said goodbye to Uncle John, Lucy, and Jaden and continued on to Okinawa. While only twice as big as Guam, Okinawa's population is almost ten times greater. Okinawa Prefecture is made up of more than a hundred and fifty distinct islands, four hundred miles from mainland Japan. The island is situated close to Taiwan and mainland China, both of which have influenced the music, food, art, and architecture just as much as Japan.

The Kadena Air Force base on Okinawa is gigantic. Hangars and matte-gray planes spread out on the tarmac for miles. Once in the terminal, everyone we encountered was American and we hailed a cab and located base lodging with ease. The taxi drove us through the base, which looked much like any other military base with American stores, American chain restaurants like McDonald's and Chili's, and American servicemen roaming the streets. I imagined a completely different world lay just outside the fence line—all signs in Japanese, unrecognizable businesses, and few Americans. We were excited to be in our first foreign country, but I'd hoped my first glimpse of Japan would look less American.

The taxi dropped us at temporary base lodging—no different than a basic hotel. We gathered our belongings and began the check-in process. Ray struck up a conversation with the front desk clerk, a young woman in crisp blues.

"Where are you from?" he asked, with a cheerful smile and wide eyes. Hours of travel and little sleep had not diminished his enthusiasm.

"Oklahoma," she replied, and smiled back at this enthusiastic man in front of her.

"How long have you been in Okinawa?" he continued.

She checked his ID and handed it back. "My husband and I have been here almost seven months now." Her smile wavered and she let out a sigh.

Forgetting many people have boundaries and oblivious to her change in demeanor, Ray launched right into a series of questions.

"Wow, seven months! Do you have any favorite restaurants? Or parks, museums, hikes? We're excited to go out and start exploring, so if you know of anything interesting in the area or if you could recommend some brochures, we'd really appreciate any advice."

When Ray paused, the clerk, without raising her eyes, answered, "I've never been off the base."

In seven months, this young woman and her husband had kept themselves confined to six square miles, encountering the same eighteen thousand Americans, shopping at the same US-stocked grocery store, eating at American restaurants, and never venturing off the base to explore the island. Not once. I would have tired of being confined to such a small area within a week. This exchange with the clerk confirmed for me that despite my fears of all the things that could possibly go wrong on this trip, my desire to see the world was much greater. I didn't want to be the girl who was too afraid to explore.

"Well, that's too bad," Ray said, not missing a beat. "I'll report back in after we explore and let you know what we find."

She smiled and thanked him.

Not deterred by the front desk clerk's lack of knowledge of the island, we hit the rental car kiosk in the hotel lobby.

"Can you tell me how much it would cost to rent a car for a day or two?" Ray asked the agent.

She tapped at her keyboard, printed out an estimate, and handed it to Ray.

"Thank you," he said. "We'll be back shortly."

As he was walking away, the clerk added, "Oh, you must have an international driver's license."

For about ten seconds, I grinned to myself in smug victory. Before the trip, Ray had challenged my insistence on getting an international driver's license, and it was coming back to bite him! The Force had failed him on this point.

In my research of world travel, I read post after post about the importance of obtaining an international driver's license. However, I never encountered information as to *why* a license was so important or the steps involved in getting one, other than to apply at your local AAA office.

Lacking specific details, my romanticized interpretation was that I'd submit all my information to AAA, and they'd send it off for translation. An official "international driver's license" with all my personal information translated into fifteen languages would then arrive in a fancy envelope four to six weeks later. I didn't stop to consider that Lisa in any other language would simply be Lisa.

Two weeks before our trip, I'd gone to the AAA office to check "international license" off my to-do list. I walked up to the agent, excited about the whole process, like the anticipation of getting my first driver's license. When I asked about what I needed to do, the agent informed me an international driver's license was a simple document indicating that I was licensed to drive a car in the United States. *That* message was translated into fifteen languages in the accompanying booklet. All I had to do was show her my current US driver's license, give her a photo and fifteen dollars, and the official international driver's license was all mine. No personal information translation, no fancy booklet, no laminated photo. Just a simple, stapled document with repeatedly photocopied words lacking the clarity of fresh type, printed on dull, heather-gray paper to further enhance the boring.

Somewhat skeptical, but concerned about checking off all my boxes and doing things right, I made the purchase. I signed the back of my picture, filled out my own information in the ugly paper booklet, and watched as the agent glued my photo to the last page and stamped across the seams so anyone looking at the document would know if it had been tampered with.

Ray teased me mercilessly when I got home, summing up what I had been feeling all along. "It's a scam. I'm glad it only cost fifteen dollars." He shook his head and rolled his eyes.

"I read so many blog posts recommending we have it," I said. "Maybe you should consider it, just in case."

He took one look at the flimsy document I had received and said, "No way."

Standing at the rental car kiosk, my triumphant grin turned to dread as I realized that if I was the only one with an international driver's license, I would have to be the one to drive the car . . . on the opposite side of the road . . . from the opposite side of the car . . . with no signs in English! My pulse began to race as I started to imagine driving.

"I'm not sure I can drive with everything backwards," I said to Ray.

"You'll be fine. I know you can do it," he said. And with that, he turned to the task of gathering brochures in search of our next adventure.

Excited to get out and explore, we didn't give much thought to anything else. After dropping our bags in our room and freshening up, we pored through the tourist brochures we'd picked up in the hotel lobby and decided the UNESCO World Heritage Site of Shuri Castle was a destination we all wanted to see. We walked back to the lobby and rented a car. The agent programmed our destination and base address into the GPS, and we took off. Never having driven in a foreign country, I was nervous about getting on the road, but at least my fears of getting lost and not being able to find our way back were eased.

Once the four of us squeezed into our sub-compact car—difficult for Tyler at 6'3"—the driving itself turned out to be fairly ordinary, as long as there were other cars I could follow at a safe distance. That first day, I only blew through a couple stop signs. In Japan, stop signs are red triangles—similar to American yield signs—and have three *kanji* characters which I had no hope of deciphering. I had no idea the characters meant stop. By the third day, I had figured out the stop signs, but I continued turning on the wipers when trying to signal left or right, because even those were on the opposite sides. My biggest trouble by far turned out to be the built-in GPS. Every time we approached a toll booth, the navigation system would sound an alarm and a starry-eyed, pink cartoon character that looked like a balloon would scream-sing at me in Japanese, warning me of the impending booth. The first time the alarm shrieked at me I almost ran off the road. I pulled up to the toll booth operator with hands shaking and offered my credit card to pay the fee.

As we drove, Ray tried some distraction. "Listen to this," he read to the boys. "The population of Okinawa is 1.5 million inhabitants and the population density is as high as eight-thousand people per square kilometer."

"What is population density?" RJ asked.

"It's how many people are in a certain amount of space. That number means there are a lot of people packed together on this small island," Ray said.

"Look at the buildings." I motioned to the buildings stacked next to one another, rising floor after floor toward the sky.

"All the cars are so small," Tyler commented.

Small smart cars dominated the roads and minivans were truly mini. Even delivery vehicles were small, resembling a toy version of their larger American counterparts. It felt as if we'd been dropped right in the middle of "miniature world."

"What's that?" RJ asked, pointing to a tower of open cubes, each with a single figure swinging a club.

"It's a driving range. Each one of those cubicles has a golfer and they're hitting balls into the colossal net," Ray said.

In the smallest of green spaces, six-story driving ranges dominated the view, squeezed between winding, noisy freeways and neighboring skyscrapers.

All along the drive, neon lights flashed signs we could not translate. There was no room for grass or trees. Vending machines offering a variety of sodas, fruit drinks, coffee products, and snacks were everywhere, occupying any open space along the roads and sidewalks.

Despite the warnings of impending toll booths, the GPS led us to our intended destination. With no street parking in sight and wishing to avoid parallel parking, I swerved into the first gated parking lot I saw. Scanning the sign at the lot entrance, I could interpret enough to know I could use a credit card or cash to pay for parking at the end of the day, although I could not decipher the rate. Looking forward to getting out of the car and away from the shrieking pink balloon, I stopped at the gate, pushed the big green button, and took my ticket. The gate lifted, welcoming us to the serenity of the lot.

We spent the afternoon exploring the castle grounds and museum. Although the exact construction date of the castle was unknown, it was in use from 1322 to 1429 when it housed King Sho Hashi. The castle burned down several times and was captured by Satsuma armies in 1609. During WWII, it was subject to three days of shelling from the USS Mississippi and ultimately captured by US forces. After the war, the castle housed a university, and in 1992, the main building was reconstructed, and the entire area dedicated as Shuri Castle Park.

I loved looking at the curved eaves of the buildings and the dragons sitting atop their peaks, whiskers twisting into the sky. The painting and carvings told a story of ancient peoples and places, far older than anything in America. The landscape watercolors detailing the craggy limestone mountains and ficus trees with multiple trunks piqued my desire to see more of this island. I left the castle in awe of all I had seen. With calmed nerves, the tension in my neck and shoulders dissipated.

On our walk back to the car, we stopped at a small café for dinner only to find no one spoke English. Relying on grainy pictures accompanied by clunky English translations, we fumbled our way through ordering—pointing, holding up fingers, and nodding when the waiter did the same. We ordered ramen noodles, purple yam donuts, fried taro and pork paste, Okinawa rice porridge, and a stir-fry tofu dish, many of the tastes and textures new to our taste buds, but everything delicious.

Tired from our day of adventure, and now with full bellies, we returned to the lot to find that the attendant booth was closed. This meant no attendant on duty to run a credit card. The only way out of the gate-secured lot was with Japanese Yen—of which, we had exactly zero. So, we set out on a new adventure to find an ATM. At the corner store adjacent to the parking lot, I stepped up to the machine, inserted my card, punched in my PIN, and waited for my cash to shoot out the front, but no cash arrived. The screen filled with Japanese text and a tiny message at the bottom in English indicating the ATM only accepted cards issued by Japanese banks.

Through another series of gestures and pointing, we got our message across to the clerk at the store—we needed cash and our card was not working. He pointed us to a nearby bank, but we had the same problem with the ATM not accepting US cards. We wandered farther down the street until we found a small grocery store, hoping we could use a debit card and get cash back. That works in the US, why not in Okinawa? Ray picked a personal size carton of ice cream and waited his turn in the checkout line.

"Can I use this card to get cash back?" Ray asked the cashier, pointing to his card.

The cashier smiled politely at Ray and bowed her head.

"Can I get Yen back if I use a debit card?" Ray tried again, his volume rising with each question, as if being louder would aid the cashier's understanding of his need.

The cashier continued to smile, but this time shook her head, obviously not understanding what Ray wanted.

"I pay for this," he held up the ice cream, "with this card," he pointed to the debit card again, "you give me Yen," he pointed at her, the cash register, and then himself with wild gestures.

Again, she shook her head. We looked around and noticed shopping in this mini market had ceased. All attention was now focused on this loud American man ranting at the cashier. People watched, unsure whether they should be amused or concerned.

"Okay, let's try it," Ray said, realizing his words were useless.

The cashier rang up the ice cream and Ray paid with his debit card, which did not give him an option of getting cash back. The boys and I grimaced with equal parts amusement and embarrassment as Ray returned to our side.

"Well, that didn't work." He handed the ice cream to the boys.

"Bitter melon?" Ty sneered in disgust.

"*Ew*," RJ agreed.

"Just give it a try," Ray said to the boys. "Any ideas?" he asked, his attention turning to me.

With no cash forthcoming and seemingly no way to get out of the parking lot, I rocked my head from side to side, the muscles in my neck tightening. The dinner I had so enjoyed now threatened to come back up. My fear that something would go wrong had become reality.

"I don't know what to do." I was at a loss for anything more.

I would guess people subject to panic attacks can remember the exact moment they experienced panic for the first time. I was twenty the first time my anxiety ballooned into a full-blown panic attack. When my living situation with my mother and Zack in Bellingham blew up, I moved back to Montana. In addition to the seven part-time jobs I was juggling to make ends meet, I also enrolled in college and signed up for a heavy load of computer engineering classes, all of which I was struggling to understand—a new experience for me since learning had always come easily. As I sat in a seminar class of a hundred students for C+ programming, the instructor began his lecture, instructing the class to turn to page 293 in the text. I dug the book out of my backpack and, in the same moment, forgot what I was supposed to be doing. I looked around and found everyone else dutifully taking notes. I didn't understand what was happening to me as a wave of panic surged through my body, causing my hands to shake. I sat frozen, feeling scattered and alone, knowing only that I had to get out of the room. I walked out in the middle of class, drove myself home, and cried myself to sleep.

For as long as I could remember, anxiety had been a pesky little nuisance. It kept me wound up in a state of worry, stressed about events and decisions others found banal. While bothersome, anxiety was something I learned to deal with and work myself out of, given enough time. I would venture to say anxiety even had some benefits. I was never late for appointments, my house was always clean, I never misplaced my keys or wallet, and I knew where everyone in my household was at any given moment of the day, due to my precise, oft-updated calendar system. I was someone who got things done.

Panic, on the other hand, continued to sneak up on me at various times throughout my life, usually when least expected. Everyone around me recognized my suffering and offered to help, but, blindsided by the attack, I couldn't even begin to form the words to let them know what I needed. Even if I could put words to my needs, they would sound foreign. Telling someone you are paralyzed with fear or that you're worked up into such a state you can barely speak or think clearly, for no obvious reason, doesn't make sense.

Through the years, panic attacks would see my body break down and rebel against me, accompanied by bouts of vomiting and diarrhea. Sleepless nights were marked by crying jags impossible to stop and lasting for days. On more than one occasion I had to seek medication to calm my mind and bring my body back into balance. Through these attacks, I learned people don't understand panic unless they, too, have had that experience. They don't understand that you can't just turn it off and that you don't want to feel this way. Panic is like having the volume turned up to maximum in every area of your physical and mental state, while everyone else in the room is unaware of the sound.

When panic subsided, I'd be angry. Angry that I couldn't control my body or my mind. Angry at my irrational behavior. Angry that I felt I had to restrict the way I lived. Angry that I'd feel drained for days afterward, walking through life in a fog. Angry that nobody understood. Angry at feeling alone. And anxious that panic could return at any time without warning.

Ray looked at me and could see the worry lining my face had grown into something bigger. "Let's head back to the car and figure out what to do," he said, his jovial manner quieting, replaced by concern.

Although dark, the night was warm. The ice cream was a welcome distraction for RJ and Tyler. They took turns taking bites as we made our way back to the car. Bitter melon apparently tasted better than it sounded. Ray and I spoke little, each of us trying to figure out what to do.

"Let's try the convenience store one more time," Ray said.

"What will that accomplish? No one speaks English."

"I don't know. Let's just try. Maybe we'll find someone who speaks English there now."

"Fine." I closed my eyes tight and wished that this mess would all just disappear.

The convenience store next to the parking lot resembled a 7-Eleven, stocked with a bit of everything. In Okinawa, however, rather than hotdogs in perpetual motion on a warming roller, every kind of sushi imaginable filled cooled cases. Shelves were laden with snacks and candy, colorful packages decorated with starry-eyed anime characters. We could sometimes identify the candy based on packaging alone, and the English name often accompanied the Japanese text on the American products. With one glance at the sweets, I remembered I had downloaded a translation app on my phone before we left. We'd had little success in our practice runs with the app, but I decided to give it a try.

I pulled out my phone and opened the app. My heart rate slowed a bit as I switched the target language to Japanese. I typed, "Car stuck in parking lot. No money. Need help." I hit the translate button, expecting this attempt to fail. Japanese characters appeared, and I showed my phone to the clerk. He stared at the letters for a bit, his face screwed up trying to decipher the message. He pointed to himself and then pointed out the door and I nodded, hoping he was indicating he would come with us.

Back in the lot, we pointed at the gate and shrugged. We couldn't even figure out how much money we needed. He pointed to us, then the car, then mimed driving the car up to the gate. We piled into the car, and I drove up to the gate. Once our car was atop the pressure plate we'd failed to notice, "¥800" flashed on an electronic screen on the attendant's booth, around $6.50. The clerk reached into his pocket, pulled out a few coins and fed them into the slot for payment. Once he reached 800 Yen, the gate opened, ushering us back onto the road. We all let out a cheer. I handed the clerk a US twenty-dollar bill, hoping he could exchange it with ease. We

thanked him profusely, and knowing he probably didn't understand, added deep head bows to make sure our message was
understood. I began the drive back to the base with a shaky
grip on the wheel.

"That was awful," I commented to no one in particular, my
nerves still throbbing.

I glanced in the mirror to check on the boys. They showed
no signs of distress. With headphones on and the blue glow of
electronics lighting their faces, they were happy to be headed
back to the hotel.

"It wasn't so bad. Everything worked out, we just hit a little
bump in the road," Ray replied.

With eyes tearing, I said, "I don't know if I can do this."

"Do what?"

"Make this trip, always feeling so out of control, I guess," I
said, biting my lip. "I panicked back there. You guys were all
calm and collected, but all I could do was think of worst-case
scenarios."

The truth was, after so many losses, my anxiety over sudden, unexpected disaster was never far from my mind. If I lost
one of my boys or Ray, my life would be unbearable. I'd be an-
nihilated by grief. Unreachable. Driving back to the base, I
wondered for a moment if anxiety and panic were hereditary.
My behavior was starting to remind me of my mother. Had she
too run up against panic so debilitating they could no longer
function in the world?

"I was a little concerned, too, but realistically, what is the
worst thing that could have happened?" Ray asked.

"I know we would have been fine, but in the moment, when
panic hits, my rational thinking is nonexistent. I can only imagine the worst."

There was no way to make Ray understand that when one of my feared scenarios happened, my brain had to work through *every* worst-case scenario in order to keep us all safe. He was the eternal optimist and took on challenges as they came up.

"We would have found a room for the night and dealt with it in the morning," Ray reasoned. "We're fine."

Yes, we were fine. He was so damn practical about everything, so levelheaded. How could I make him understand the depth of panic I experienced in that moment?

"We were dumb." I gave him a sidelong glance. "We didn't even think to get Yen. That's pretty basic, and we managed to screw it up."

"Rookie mistake. Now we know better."

"What happens next time when the bump isn't so minor? What happens when things go really wrong?"

Ray exhaled. "We'll be together, and we'll figure it out. These are the kinds of situations we are going to encounter, and we'll get through it."

"I don't know."

I still feared I was somehow being irresponsible dragging my kids around the world, especially when I was feeling far from put together. There would be bumps along the way. That was part of international travel. But I hated feeling out of control. I had always been so sure of myself, knowing just what to do and when, and willing to face whatever issue I encountered in my life. Now I was out of my comfort zone and freaking out at the smallest of mishaps. Without the numbing effect of alcohol, my feelings were amplified. Everything felt more intense.

Our conversation for the rest of the drive was light, a superficial commentary on the sights and sounds of Okinawa. I crawled into bed that night wondering if we should turn back and head home. But something inside wouldn't let me go there. Turning back was not the answer. If I left this adventure now, I knew I would feel like a failure for the rest of my life. I imagined people asking, "What made you come back so soon?" My reply of calling the whole thing off because I was stuck in a parking lot for a couple of hours sounded ridiculous, even to my ears. I could picture the looks on their faces, questioning, skeptical, judging. I was ashamed of myself, just thinking about such a conversation. I had to deal with setbacks and learn how to solve problems rather than run from them.

I put my headphones on and started an audiobook to ease me into sleep, my only method for falling asleep since The Glitch began. Weariness demanded sleep, but sleep meant dreams, and after years marked by death and dying, dreams held only nightmares. You don't get a good night's sleep when surrounded by death. You don't eat or drink or work or play or shop or even breathe the same as you did before the nightmares. I needed the distraction of a fictional reality to calm my thoughts and allow my brain to shut down. I hoped sleep would ease the anxieties of the day and get me started in a better place in the morning. I drifted off, thankful the day's adventure had come to an end and I was in an actual bed rather than a parked car.

The next morning, armed with enough Japanese currency to get us out of the most exclusive parking lot in Okinawa, procured from the air base ATM, we set out to find a place where we could escape the cramped, miniature-filled city. We headed to the less populated, northern side of Okinawa, dominated by expanses of natural forests rather than concrete jungles. Our hour-and-a-half drive took us along the western edge of Okinawa where we caught our first views of the East China Sea.

This brilliant, glowing blue water was so alluring I pulled the car over to marvel at its beauty. The rhythm of the waves and warm ocean breeze infiltrated my senses and reinforced a sense of calm. Not having toll booths and a shrieking pink balloon along the way helped, too.

We made our way to Hiji Falls National Park and set off on a short hike along a winding path and a series of stairs meandering up and down the steep landscape. The forest was alive with cicadas but otherwise fairly bug-free. The park was also mostly human-free, which suited our desire to be away from crowds. Our trail led to a suspension bridge spanning a river sixty feet below, and ultimately to Hiji Waterfall, a ninety-foot veil of water cascading over enormous, jagged rocks. As we rested our aching leg muscles, hypnotized by the never-ending flow of water, I thought of the hotel clerk. Keeping herself sequestered on base, she would probably never taste authentic Japanese foods, glimpse the brilliance of the East China Sea, experience a piece of Okinawa history, or bask in the grandeur and beauty of a natural world entirely different from what she knew. I couldn't help but wonder if she might understand my fears.

Coming down from the hike, we were all ready for a little refreshment. Although we were flush with money, the opposite was true for potable water. The trail ended at a rustic, dilapidated outhouse with two pristine vending machines at one end, incongruous in this natural setting. Inside each vending machine, an array of fruit- and cola-flavored drinks and bright multicolored cans of coffee, each bearing Tommy Lee Jones' image in profile, sat chilled and ready for purchase.

"Well, that *is* convenient," I joked, nudging my elbow in Ray's ribs.

"Leave it to the Japanese to put a vending machine exactly where you might want one," Ray added.

We sat at a picnic bench sipping on fizzy drinks in cans decorated with colorful fruits, flowers, and indecipherable text, and cold Tommy Lee Jones' Boss coffee. This day had brought no misadventures, only a beautiful drive along the South China Sea leading us to an incredible hike. Had I turned back after the parking lot incident, I never would have been able to see the beauty of this remote area of Okinawa. And with that thought, I knew I had made the decision to continue the journey. What adventures would I miss if we turned back? What would I regret *not* seeing? The world was full of wonders I wanted to experience firsthand. Would things go off track again at some point? Probably. Wouldn't we also make memories and have experiences we'd talk about for the rest of our lives? Definitely. The decision to continue to face the trials of travel would have been a no-brainer before The Glitch. I realized I was fighting for the smallest amount of control anywhere I could, even when situations were beyond my control. I knew I still had to find a balance. And turning back was not the answer.

"What are we doing tomorrow?" RJ asked.

Ray glanced at me, waiting for me to take the lead.

"I really enjoyed today. I feel like maybe I could get used to having adventures." My mind was calm. I knew I wanted to continue even with obstacles certain to come.

Ray smiled knowingly. "You sure?"

"I know we'll probably have some hiccups along the way, but I'd rather take my chances now than find myself years down the road too old to travel, filled with regret. I know we were stuck for a while, but we saw some pretty cool things, too."

"It was just a parking lot, Mom," Tyler added. I smiled at the easy wisdom of my fourteen-year-old son but wondered if he understood how anxious I had been.

Yep. It was just a parking lot. Get over it.

None of the obstacles we encountered in Okinawa were in-surmountable. Some might even conclude they were trivial. Part of saying *yes* to the adventure meant I would need to learn to sit back and let the adventure unfold.

When we returned to the base, the seventy-two-hour flight schedule listed a flight to Singapore with forty-seven seats for the next day.

"What does everyone think about Singapore?" Ray asked.

"I thought we were going to South Korea," Tyler said.

"Where is Singapore?" RJ asked.

"When we were watching the schedules back home, there were a lot of flights from Okinawa to South Korea, so we thought that might be our next hop, but we were just guessing based on history," I explained.

"Singapore is south of Malaysia," Ray added to answer RJ.

"If we go to Singapore, we won't have to fly commercial to mainland Asia, which could save us a lot of money. But we had planned to get to North Vietnam and then travel south." My mind was abuzz with all the new complications this change would cause. "Singapore will definitely change those plans. Will we travel north instead?" I asked.

"I don't know," Ray said. "I say we head to Singapore and figure things out as we go. You all right with that?"

He was so calm in that moment. I tried to relax into the thought of taking it one step at a time.

I nodded. "Okay. Let's do it." The idea scared me. I hadn't planned on Singapore, but I was committed to the journey and keeping panic at bay. I just had to remember to deal with one obstacle at a time. I would not be the girl who was afraid.

Days of Travel: 30
Miles Logged: 8,757

BLESSED

Singapore, Singapore

"I need to warn you that the air quality in Singapore is in the unhealthy range now, due to the fires in Indonesia." Everything about this young woman was serious—her pressed blue uniform, hair knotted at the base of her neck, the slight pinch of skin between her eyebrows. "Is Singapore your final destination?" she asked, as she reviewed our passports and travel orders.

I didn't think she would be one to endure a long explanation, but the answer was not a simple yes or no. How could we explain succinctly that we didn't know where we were going or how long we'd stay? That the whole trip up to this point had been based on chance and where Space-A flights took us? That I was trying really hard to remain calm and her warnings about Singapore being unhealthy weren't helping?!

"For this leg of the trip, it is," I said. "We're actually taking several months to travel around the world. We never imagined we'd get all the way to Singapore."

With no American military bases on mainland Asia, our primary goal at the beginning of the trip had been to get as close to Asia as possible on military flights and then fly the rest of the way on commercial planes. From Okinawa, we had hoped to get to either the Philippines or South Korea. Though neither location was located on mainland Asia, both islands had major airports that could get us to Vietnam. A flight to Singapore would mean one less commercial flight we'd have to take.

"We've seen a bit of news coverage on the fires, but I thought they were mostly in Indonesia," Ray said.

"Indonesia is about seven-hundred miles to the south, but the smoke is affecting air quality in Singapore and neighboring countries. Are you sure you want to get on the flight?" she repeated.

"Definitely," Ray said, his enthusiasm never wavering.

Making it all the way to mainland Asia on military flights translated into a huge cost savings for us.

"How smoky could it be?" I asked Ray in a whisper when the agent turned away.

He shrugged. "I think I heard about them canceling the Formula One race there."

"Here is a list of rules to follow in Singapore." The agent turned back toward us and handed Ray a piece of paper. "I need to advise you to read through the list carefully. You will also want to read the list to everyone in your party."

"Will do," said Ray, handing me the list of rules.

Singapore is among the twenty smallest countries in the world, with a total land area of only two hundred and sixty-three square miles. In comparison, Hawaii's Big Island is fifteen times larger. Singapore is one of only three surviving city-states in the world—sort of a small, independent country with a single city. The other two are Monaco and Vatican City.

We settled into hard, plastic chairs in the waiting area and I pulled out the list of rules.

"Okay, boys, listen up. We need to review the rules of Singapore." I waved the paper for everyone to see.

"I heard you can't chew gum there," Ty chimed in.

"These rules look a little more serious. Ready?" I said. "First, no selling gum. That one carries a hundred thousand dollar fine or two years in prison."

"What!? A hundred thousand dollars? American dollars?" asked Tyler. A hundred thousand dollars was an absurd amount of money for a teen boy.

"Why would we sell gum?" RJ asked.

Trying to get the facts sorted out, Ty asked, "But can we chew gum, right?"

"I'm not sure why you would sell it. It sounds like they don't like gum-chewers, so I would probably avoid gum altogether while we're there." I tried to answer all the questions flying at me. "Next, a thousand dollar fine for annoying someone by playing a musical instrument. Oh, finally, a rule that will end Dad's singing!" I said, winking in Ray's direction.

"Are you saying my voice is a musical instrument? That's so kind. I knew you secretly liked my singing!" Ray beamed.

RJ, Tyler, and I groaned. The only admirers of Ray's singing were neighborhood dogs who all perked up and added to the chorus when Ray belted out a tune.

"Let's keep going. There's a five thousand dollar fine for flying a kite or playing any game that interferes with public traffic," I continued. "Three months in prison, a fine, or both, for singing or uttering songs that have obscene lyrics."

"Ha! I can sing," Ray said.

"But, please don't, Dad," Tyler added, making us all laugh.

"All right, c'mon everyone, let's finish the list," I said. "A thousand dollar fine for spitting in any public place."

"Spitting on the ground, or anywhere? What if you spit your gum in a garbage can, does that count?" Tyler asked, always trying to define the letter of the law.

"I think we just avoid gum," Ray answered.

I mouthed a silent "thank you" in his direction.

"Connecting to another user's Wi-Fi is deemed as hacking and carries a ten thousand dollar fine, three years in prison, or both." I could see both boys trying to work out what exactly this meant for their online pursuits and how they might get around the restriction.

"Listen to this one, boys. All boys," I said. "Forgetting to flush the toilet is a hundred and fifty dollar fine." I looked at each of them in turn and wondered if I could institute a similar policy in my own home.

"Who goes around checking that?" Ray asked.

"We're almost done." The seriousness of the list was dissolving fast. "No feeding the pigeons. That one comes with a five hundred dollar fine. And no urinating in a public elevator. This says some public elevators have urine detection devices that trigger an alarm and close the doors until the police arrive when any odor of urine is detected."

"Urinating? You mean peeing?" RJ asked.

"Yep. No peeing in an elevator," I said, as the boys looked at each other quizzically and then erupted in giggles.

"All right, all right, two more. No jaywalking. That one is twenty dollars on the spot or it could be a thousand dollar fine or three months in jail. And the fines double if you're caught twice. Finally, no taking drugs before you enter the country. That one carries a twenty thousand dollar fine, ten years in prison, or, in certain cases, the death penalty." I finished reading and put the list down.

"Again, who is checking? Do we have to give blood and urine samples when we enter the country?" Ray asked with a roll of his eyes.

"Just make sure you're not in an elevator when you give your sample," I said.

The list sounded manageable, but I was hit with a little pang of anxiety thinking about what other laws there might be and envisioning the consequences of breaking the rules.

We easily made the flight, since only seven passengers, including our family of four, showed up to claim one of the forty-seven available seats. We boarded the plane and took off for this small island nation at the base of Malaysia, eighty-eight miles north of the equator, essentially the southernmost point of continental Asia. Spread out along the cargo-net seats, our backpacks cinched together on a pallet in the center of the plane, we settled in for the seven-hour flight. Although physically comfortable nestled into the cargo net, my head resting on a balled-up sweatshirt, my thoughts were spiraling as I looked around at the empty plane. The lack of passengers made me feel like maybe everyone else knew something I didn't, and the agent's repeated question kept looping in my mind, "Are you sure you want to get on the flight?" I had not done any research on Singapore, and with few other passengers on the plane and a list of obscure rules that we had to follow, I felt unsure about our quick decision to leap blindly to this unknown nation.

Landing in Singapore, the plane was engulfed by the thickest brown smoke I had ever seen. Although only midday, the haze choked the sun's rays and made it feel like late evening. Before exiting the plane, we were again warned air quality ranked in the "very unhealthy" range. A wall of humidity and smoke blasted us as we exited the plane. The air was so thick I could feel the grime accumulate on my skin. The blanket of dense air sapped our energy and left us all struggling to get enough oxygen as we walked across the tarmac. I was approaching panic stage, worried we'd made the wrong decision in coming here.

The terminal itself was a tiny, walk-in-closet-sized room. Three chairs lined one wall and a small teller window housing passport control sat open at one end. As we waited for our luggage to come in from the plane, I looked around for a Traveler Information Sheet—a listing of recommended places to stay and dine in the area. I had grown accustomed to finding the sheets in all the US military terminals we had visited. I only then remembered this was not a US installation. The Paya Lebar Air Base belonged to the Singapore Air Force and was utilized by various flying units of the US military for refueling stops and staging points.

Since we hadn't expected to get to Singapore, we had failed to make hotel reservations. The lack of preparation along with the oppressive smoke and humidity ramped up my anxiety. When we'd landed in Okinawa, the base personnel had been primarily American. This was not the case in Singapore. The familiar comfort of US terminals was nonexistent—no place to lounge while waiting for flights, no air conditioning, and no helpful information sheet. For the first time, four weeks into our trip, we would have to rely on ourselves with no support from base personnel or anyone else.

As the luggage finished unloading, only two of our four backpacks were brought into the terminal. Our luggage had been right in front of us for the entire flight. The plane was parked less than a hundred feet from the terminal and somehow, in that hundred feet, our luggage had been misplaced.

Regulations prohibited us from carrying our own bags off the plane, but I was sure even my two teenage sons could have kept track of their packs for that long.

I felt my anxiety intensify. Once again, we had nowhere to stay, and now, two of us would be stuck in the clothes we were wearing.

"How could they lose our luggage? What are we going to do?" I asked, my voice booming in this undersized terminal space. "My phone isn't set up for Singapore yet. I can't get online to look anything up. We have nowhere to stay and two of our bags are missing!" Passengers' heads were turning, sensing, even if not totally understanding, the alarm in my voice.

"Stop getting so worked up," Ray snapped. Sweat dripping down his face, he was clearly feeling the effects of the heat and smoke. "One step at a time."

As we made our way through passport control, our missing backpacks were located.

"Now what do we do?" I asked.

"Just sit for a minute and I'll go see what I can find." Ray pointed to the open chairs.

I sat, leaned my head back, and closed my eyes, making a conscious effort to breathe deeply in and out and quiet the heightened clamor in my mind. Was anxiety one of the five stages of grief?

Ray returned a few minutes later and told us he'd found a hotel and had made reservations for the night. We simply had to walk off the base to meet the taxi. We trudged into this apocalyptic-feeling, sweltering foreign land through barricaded gates flanked by Singaporean soldiers armed with automatic rifles.

Outside the gates, I stood on the sidewalk watching the cars rush by on the busy city street, not unlike any other bustling city traffic. If not for the haze from the smoke, this could have been any other suburb with storefronts open at the street level of four-story buildings, apartments occupying the remaining floors. Beads of sweat streamed down my back, and my throat ached with each inhalation of polluted air. I was sure I'd never been so hot, like a fire was raging just under the surface of my skin. Within minutes a taxi pulled over to pick us up. The driver loaded our backpacks in the trunk and whisked us into Singapore.

"You want Princess Hotel?" the driver asked with raised eyebrows.

"Yes. That's the one," Ray replied.

"You take boys there?" the driver asked, nodding toward the backseat where I was with Tyler and RJ.

"Yes, all of us," Ray said.

I should have been a little suspicious something was amiss based on the driver's question, but I was too busy looking at our new environment to notice. In this tropical climate, paint seemed to bubble and peel off every building, old or new, giving them all a shabby, rundown look. But with shops open and people bustling about, the only difference between this and any other city was that all the writing was in a language we had no hope of decoding.

As the boys and I unloaded our backpacks and headed toward the hotel entrance, I saw the taxi driver pull Ray aside and whisper something in his ear. We entered the ordinary lobby and began the check-in process, handing over passports and filling out registration cards.

"What did he say?" I asked Ray, who was all of a sudden uncharacteristically quiet.

He avoided looking directly at me. "He said this was the red-light district of the city."

"Seriously? Is it safe here?"

"Very safe area," the hotel clerk chimed in. "All of Singapore safe, very little crime."

"It'll be educational," said Ray, in his typical optimistic fashion. "We can teach the boys what's meant by 'red-light districts.'"

I rolled my eyes but didn't put up an argument. Any slight sense of well-being faded when I found the mattresses covered with plastic sheets.

"How did you find this place exactly?" I asked Ray as I unpacked my sleep sheet—there was no way I'd be sleeping directly on the plastic sheets.

"I asked the guys at the terminal. Maybe they think this is what American guys are looking for," Ray said, shrugging his shoulders.

After stowing our belongings, we stopped at the front desk to ask for recommendations on a place to eat. "There are many good places on main street to the left." The clerk pointed in the direction of a busy street.

"And you're sure it's safe to walk?" I asked, seeking more reassurance.

"Yes. Singapore is safe. This is the red-light district, but not dangerous. Prostitution is legal here," he responded.

"Okay, let's go." I wasn't sure if that statement made me feel any better. Ray held the door open for us and we turned for the main street a couple of blocks away.

"What's a red-light district?" Tyler asked once outside.

Ray looked at me with raised eyebrows.

"Nope, you can take this one," I said.

Ray was quiet for a moment. "Well, typically it's where you find a lot of taverns and seedy people, where you'd go to hire a mercenary," he tried.

I rolled my eyes. "I don't think that quite hits the mark." I looped my arm through his, letting him guide me while I stayed alert and on the lookout for anything I felt might be out of the ordinary.

"What's a mercenary?" RJ asked.

"Try again," I said, amused.

"A red-light district is home to the oldest profession on the planet . . . prostitution," Ray began, deciding on an academic approach. "Where women, and sometimes men, make their living by having sex with people." He paused, anticipating questions. The boys continued looking straight ahead, perhaps wondering if there was any more to it.

When no questions came, Ray continued, "In a lot of places around the world, prostitution is illegal, but not here. And there is really no reason it should be. Making prostitution illegal actually makes it more dangerous."

"How does it make it more dangerous?" Tyler asked.

I was happy to know they were listening, even if Ray's explanation was somewhat abstract.

"Well, at my job, there are rules in place to keep everyone safe and healthy. But since prostitution is illegal, the women don't have health insurance and if they are hurt on the job, they cannot take legal action because their job itself is illegal."

All conversation stopped as we walked past a beautiful woman dressed in a short red dress and stiletto heels. She smiled and gave us a little wave. Wandering through the red-light district, listening to my husband give a PG-rated talk on prostitution, I smiled to myself. This was the over-the-top personality I'd fallen in love with so many years ago.

Ray had come bounding into my life one day as I was playing volleyball in the park. With his limitless enthusiasm and positive attitude, he was quickly accepted into the group and we became fast friends. While he wasn't really my type, I enjoyed his enthusiasm and the way he lightened my spirits. Although my friends and family said I should consider dating Ray, I wasn't ready to head down that path. I thought he was far too much of a goofball to romantically involve myself with him, and I was happy to keep him locked in the friend zone. I had always pictured myself with more of a Brad Pitt in *A River Runs Through It*, throw me over his shoulder and carry me off to his cabin in the woods, sexy Montana mountain man. This skinny dentist with his half-mullet, military-issued eyeglasses, and affinity for *Star Wars* wasn't the man I'd pictured spending the rest of my life with.

Instead, Ray and I concocted a scheme to aid each other in getting dates with other volleyball players we'd been admiring. I would invite the girl Ray liked on a camping trip and Ray would invite the guy I liked. We imagined a fabulous beach weekend where the four of us would sit by the campfire, frolic in the waves, and fall in love under the stars. Unfortunately, the girl flaked at the last minute and we ended up being an awkward threesome for the weekend. Sparks flew for two of us, but Ray was left out of the picture.

Less than a year later, that same guy I fell in love with under the stars dumped me out of the blue and broke my heart. Ray lent me a shoulder and comforted me as I sobbed into the wee hours of the morning.

After my breakup, Ray and I spent even more time together. We enjoyed long weekend hikes, playing volleyball, and watching movies. Friends and family again whispered we should date, that we were perfect for each other. Skeptical, and not recovered from the last romantic failure, I loved having this new best friend in my life and I didn't want to screw it up by sleeping with him.

On a clear night in August, Ray and I planned to walk to a nearby park to catch a glimpse of the Perseid meteor shower. When I arrived at Ray's condo, I realized I had forgotten my sweatshirt. The evening was cool, so I asked to borrow one of his. We walked to the park, spread out a blanket, and stared up at the heavens in search of shooting stars. With little action in the sky, Ray dozed off. I listened to his light snore mixed with the waves lapping on the rocks, until the breeze off the water turned cold. When I started to shiver, I nudged Ray to wake him. Still groggy, he turned over on his side and gently laid one hand on my cheek. "Are you cold? What time is it?"

Although shocked by his touch, I chalked it up to him waking from a dream and did not consider the gesture any further. We walked back up the hill and Ray escorted me to my car. I returned his sweatshirt, said goodnight, and pulled out of the parking spot without another thought. As I stopped at the intersection, I looked in the rearview mirror one last time. Ray closed his eyes and slowly brought the sweatshirt to his face as if to breathe me in. My heart skipped a beat and my stomach filled with butterflies. I knew in that instant Ray was "the one." He was a match for me intellectually. He challenged me in all the right ways and made me laugh and take myself far less seriously. He was my equal in sarcasm, he would always be my best friend, and I knew he would always love me passionately. Even if he didn't look like Brad Pitt.

Listening to Ray finish up his talk on prostitution, I smiled and continued walking, feeling content. I hadn't thought of that moment in a long time.

Proud of himself for tackling that parenting hurdle, Ray said, "See, that wasn't so bad, was it?"

"Uh huh." I laughed. "But you never get to make hotel reservations again."

I scolded myself for having been so anxious and unable to function under pressure. Things were turning out fine. The only strain was coming from within.

As the hotel clerk had predicted, we were completely safe walking around this area of Singapore and our dinner was exceptionally ordinary. Other than placing our order by iPad, that is. We would later learn Singapore ranks near the top for digital infrastructure and boasts free Wi-Fi throughout the city. I was relieved there would be no fine for hacking on this trip.

We woke the next morning determined to see more of Singapore. Although the smog choked the sun's rays, temperatures still hovered in the nineties, and humidity climbed toward ninety percent. Our clothes were damp with perspiration as soon as we walked out the door and into a stew of smoke. We took a cab downtown to get a view of the Marina Bay Sands Hotel and the Merlion fountain, iconic features of the city. The Merlion is the official mascot of Singapore, a mythical creature with a lion's head and the body of a fish. The fountain sits across the bay from the Marina Bay Sands Hotel, a jet from its mouth constantly spraying into the water.

I had hoped to be able to visit the hotel's SkyPark, located atop its towers. But as we looked across the bay through a cloud of smoky haze, that thought faded. No sense paying for a nonexistent view. Instead, we admired from afar the three seven-hundred-foot towers topped by a giant, ship-like structure and read a description of the hotel on a placard near the fountain—more than twenty-five hundred rooms, a museum, a mall, two theaters, celebrity chef restaurants, art and science exhibits, and an atrium casino with five hundred tables and sixteen hundred slot machines.

We decided to take a short walk around the bay to see what else we could discover in Singapore. As we strolled along, Ray read the placards aloud. Self-coined the "Garden City," we learned that Singapore promoted and, in new developments, required inclusion of green spaces in the form of green roofs, cascading vertical gardens, and lush living walls. The boys and I looked at the skyscrapers surrounding the bay and found that many had balconies decked with trees and shrubs; entrances displayed living garden walls from floor to ceiling; and on smaller buildings thriving gardens sprouted from rooftops. Due to its small size, Singapore had no choice but to adopt high-density development, but the illusion of space was added with interspersed parks, rivers, and ponds amid the high-rise buildings. Even through the haze, the green spaces added a scenic quality to the city.

As we made our way to the Singapore Botanic Gardens, the rain began. Being from the Pacific Northwest, we were no strangers to rain. But tropical rain differs completely from the intermittent drizzle we were used to. When it rains in the tropics, rivers of water flood from the sky. By the time our taxi dropped us at the garden entrance, lightning and thunder was cracking all around us. Due to the proximity of the lightning, we could not enter the gardens until the storm had passed, but instead we were directed to wait under a large, open-air shelter with no walls and a simple thatched roof. Looking up, I was skeptical of the protection this roof could offer from lightning. The thatched roof seemed far from adequate. We took a seat on a bench as far away from the edge of the shelter as possible and watched as lightning flashed all around us, followed by deafening thunder.

"Mom, look at my arms!" Ty said. Every hair on his arms stood on end and I could feel the hair on my arms doing the same.

"Holy shit!" Ray burst out as another flash of lightning struck just outside the shelter. A crack of ear-splitting thunder vibrated through our bodies less than a second later.

"Dad, no swearing." RJ wore a worried look.

"Oh my God!" I said, my heart racing.

Our exclamations had drawn the attention of a neatly dressed Asian man.

"The planes made rain," he said, looking at our family.

"A plane?" I asked, not sure if this calm fellow had chosen the right words.

"The smoke is so bad, the planes put chemicals in the clouds to force rain. Rain helps clear the smoke," he replied. Nope, his English was pretty good.

Never having heard of such a thing, we asked a few more questions and learned that the air quality had gotten so bad in Singapore, officials had decided to seed the clouds. Airplanes flew above the smoke and dispersed chemical substances into the air to increase precipitation and provide relief from the smoke. Fascinated as I was at the science behind cloud seeding, all I could imagine were chemicals raining down on us.

Singapore's neighboring country of Indonesia had struggled for years to contain forest fires—the result of illegal slash-and-burn practices to clear land and make way for new plantations to fuel the lucrative palm oil industry. The haze and smoke had engulfed Singapore, Malaysia, and even reached three thousand miles north, to the tip of southern Thailand.

We'd heard snippets about the fires in Indonesia on the news before we left the US, but this was a firsthand look at the fire's far-reaching effects. Sitting on the couch half a world away watching a thirty-second news clip does little to aid one's understanding of such a catastrophic event. These fires had been raging for more than two months. We had the ability to escape the fires, but in Singapore, people were dying due to respiratory issues and hundreds of thousands of people in several countries had no choice but to live with the consequences of another nation's actions. This crisis would later be dubbed the "Southeast Asian Haze."

And yet, even in the smoke, we chose to seek out the beauty Singapore had to offer. Before we could ask any more questions, the storm let up and the crowd that had gathered under the shelter set out to tour the Singapore Botanic Garden. The National Orchid Garden—a main attraction within the park—displayed over one thousand species and two thousand hybrids of orchid in every color imaginable. Flowers dominated every space in the park and my thoughts drifted to my mom.

She was passionate about adorning her space with flowers. She had installed a series of containers along a side wall of her porch and every summer the pots overflowed with flowers, transforming the space into a living flower wall.

"You know who would have loved this place?" I said to Ray and the boys.

"Grandma," Ty answered.

Having been a professional photographer for many years, Mom also enjoyed taking photos of flowers. She would often enlarge photos into full-size canvas prints and give them as gifts or hang them in her home. Her favorite was a close-up of a white lily set against a blurred backdrop of red roses which she insisted on hanging in the guestroom of my house, where she spent the final weeks of her life.

Over the years, it became a Mother's Day tradition for me to give Mom a hanging fuchsia with cascading tendrils of vivid purple and red blossoms streaming over the pot. She would hang the plant on the corner of her deck railing and admire the hummingbirds it attracted. On her final Mother's Day, thinking she might be tired of fuchsias, I presented Mom with a large pot filled with a rainbow of flowers. I set up the pot on my kitchen table and planned for her to find it upon our return from brunch.

"Come this way." I led her to the dining room.

She hadn't noticed the flowers on my dining room table, so I prodded, "Look. These are for you."

"What's this?" she asked, her lips pressed tight.

"It's for you, happy Mother's Day."

She looked at the flowers, and with an upturned nose, said, "Hmm. No fuchsia this year?" as she slid the pot across the table, the pot scratching a deep gouge in the wood. She eyed the flowers, her expression one of superiority.

My heart sank, and I was speechless. No matter what I tried, it never seemed to be enough—I wasn't enough—to fill the void Zack's death had created. Though our relationship had not been all bad, Zack's death and her illness were suffocating whatever good was left.

Rather than enjoying the elegant and vibrant flowers dominating every space in the park, I felt like I was suffocating in my own hazy cloud of negativity by replaying the final weeks of Mom's life.

As if reading my mind, Tyler sighed and said, "Can we be done with flowers?"

"Yes, let's get out of here." I was ready to move on. I wanted to leave the memory of the flowers and the memory of my mom behind.

Our next stop was the Buddha Tooth Relic Temple and Museum, which claimed to house the left canine tooth of Buddha, recovered from his funeral pyre in Kushinagar, India. While the boys and I were unconvinced this museum would hold our interest, there was no way we could pass up a temple dedicated to a tooth when traveling with a dentist.

Thousands of artifacts and a plethora of information about Buddha were contained in this five-story red pagoda. We wound our way from floor to floor, reading a detailed history of Buddha. I found a statue of my personal guardian deity based on my zodiac sign and the year of my birth. The accompanying sign read: *A personal guardian deity serves as a source of solace, spiritual support, and inspiration. Simply having a personal guardian deity is not enough, however. One must actively work on purifying negative tendencies and increasing our store of merit and wisdom in order to strengthen our connection to our deity and speed our progress on a spiritual path.*

I'd never thought about purifying negative thoughts and tendencies; I'd just been carrying on with my life, allowing negativity to dominate my thinking and behavior. Actively working on letting in the positive and flushing the negative required a radical shift in my thinking.

I'd had experience with death before The Glitch and had managed in a typical way. But the series of deaths of close family members kept grief at the forefront of my thoughts, never allowing the healing process to begin. The emotions meant to be temporary staked their claim on my mental processing and hunkered down for the long haul. The more I thought about this purification, the more I understood this was really what I needed.

When we reached the highest floor of the temple, we were asked to remove our shoes and place our belongings in a locker before entering the shrine holding the tooth of Buddha. We stepped over the threshold to find a large room flanked by meditation spaces on both sides, and individual meditation nooks taking up the center of the room. Walking down an aisle on either side of the room led to a glassed-off area the size of a small bedroom, completely covered in gold. A giant stupa made from seven hundred pounds of gold sat in the center of the room. Right in the middle of this gleaming shrine was a miniature gold pavilion which housed the tooth of Buddha. Or so we were told.

We all stood staring into the golden housing, searching for anything resembling a tooth.

"Where is it?" RJ whispered.

I looked to Ray, certain a dentist would be able to identify the tooth. "Is that it right in the middle?" I asked.

"I think so," said Ray. "But it looks big, more like a molar."

"You *think* so?" I asked, giggling a little.

As we all stood trying to positively identify the tooth, a museum guide approached and led us to a monk who had been sitting in meditation in the corner of the room. I was initially hesitant, certain we were being reprimanded for being too loud, but the guide indicated he wanted to sing a blessing for us.

The monk was dressed in the traditional Buddhist triple saffron robe and had a necklace of large brown beads strung around his neck, reaching almost to his waist. He greeted us with palms pressed together and a gentle bow. Not having been raised in a religious household, I was nervous. What should I do with my hands? Would I need to repeat any lines like I'd heard in Catholic ceremonies?

Incense sticks burning in a small pot produced a sweet haze in the corner of the room where the monk stood. He did not speak, but looked at each of us directly for a long moment. His gaze, along with his beatific smile, put me at ease, like a weight had been lifted off my chest and I could breathe a little easier. I sensed the monk looked directly at me longer and with more intensity. I looked back at his eyes, not wanting to break the connection. I felt as if he could see inside my soul and could feel the intimacies of my struggle and the heartache I'd experienced.

The monk turned his head toward the guide and nodded. The guide asked us to kneel on the bare wood floor. The monk then picked up strands of beads like his own and placed one around each of our necks while the guide asked us to speak our names aloud. The monk again looked at each of us in turn as we spoke our names. He then knelt in front of us and began to sing a blessing in a language that was foreign, soft, and melodic.

The pain in my knees faded as the singing mingled with my thoughts. It made perfect sense that if I didn't replace negative thoughts, they'd make a home in my mind and become harder and harder to eliminate. If I wanted to break up the negative cloud in my brain, I would have to work at it. I would need my own, non-toxic version of cloud seeding to clear the smoke and make way for the sun. I began to understand I was in charge of this process and change would not occur overnight.

Still kneeling on the hard floor, the song started to lose clarity in my mind, replaced by an ache in my knees. My legs started to tremble slightly, and I felt light-headed. And just as my thoughts shifted back to my physical being, the blessing ended. The monk smiled and bowed, his head almost touching the floor. We returned the bow and thanked him. The guide collected our beads and led us back to the tooth shrine, where he directed us to meditate for a few minutes. We stood quietly in this holy space, alone with our thoughts.

"Mom, what are we doing?" RJ asked, unsure about the rules of meditating.

Wanting another moment of contemplation, I replied, "Just be quiet for a sec and think about the song the monk was singing."

Although my answer was an attempt to give myself a few more minutes of contemplation, I hoped this also might be the

best way to impart meditation to RJ. I didn't know how to interpret the song, but I knew something had changed within me. I
felt like I knew what I needed to do. I had to keep moving forward and stop replaying messages from the past. I had to practice staying present in the current moment and enjoy this time
with my family, right now. Not in an effort to forget my loved
ones who had died; that would never happen. But to honor the
people with whom I was with, and myself—shift my attention
from the negative thoughts to the present experience.

Looking awkward as he tried not to appear disrespectful,
Tyler asked, "Have we meditated long enough?"

I looked at Ray. "Are you still trying to find the tooth?"

"Actually, I was wondering if the monk has to shave his
head every day," Ray said.

The boys and I tried to suppress our laughter. "C'mon, let's
go." With a nod toward the door, I led the way out and we
made our way back to the hotel.

I went to bed that night wrapped in my sleep blanket on top
of plastic sheets in the red-light district of this smoky nation
feeling at ease in the world, like I had glimpsed a way through
the grief and back to normality. I could see there was a way
through my cloud of negativity and grief—a way to not only
temper the smoke but put out the fires completely.

Singapore had opened my eyes to the idea of thinking about
things in a different way, actively working on clearing negativity and working toward peace. But knowing and practicing
were two different things. Awareness alone did not clear the
haze built up inside me. It would take time, effort, and practice
to figure out how to seed the clouds of rage, resentment, control, and perfection in a way to help them dissipate.

I woke up the next morning and rolled onto my side, the
plastic sheets crunching beneath my sleep sack as I turned to

stare out the window into the brown haze. The smell of wet plaster permeated the room. As miserable as this situation might look to an outside observer, I felt a lightness that had been missing before. I still wasn't totally at ease in this grungy hotel room, but I didn't feel the need to crawl into a dark corner and hide away from the world, either.

As I slowly worked my way out of dreamland, I wished for a moment that simply reading about purifying negative thoughts or hearing the words sung by the monk had triggered some shift in my thinking, that my subconscious brain could decipher the message and normalcy would return on its own. But I knew it wouldn't be that easy. Maybe, just maybe, though, it was The Force pointing me in the right direction.

As we searched for breakfast along a row of hawker stations, I asked Ray how he was feeling about the trip so far.

"Honestly," he said, "I wasn't sure we'd make it this far. I thought it might be too much."

"Do I seem any different to you?"

"I think you've been able to let things go. You seem happier"—he shot me a playful smile—"and you're not so hard to get along with."

I knew he was joking, but there was some truth to his statement, too.

"Do you feel like something's changed for you?" he added, stopping to turn toward me.

My gaze fell to the ground. "I was really unhappy at home. I had no time to cope with one death before there was another." I looked up at him and continued, "The last two years with Mom took a toll on my resilience, more than I even want to admit."

I felt vulnerable saying this out loud, like I was letting Ray see the ugliest parts of me. But he held my gaze with the same quality of attention as the monk, and I felt a sense of familiarity return, enough to continue. "She broke my spirit. Made me feel like nothing. I think I only survived by drinking and shutting it all out. Our relationship suffered the consequences."

He nodded but didn't say anything. Instead, he took my hand and we kept walking. We continued by the food stalls, hanging back, while keeping RJ and Tyler in sight. Ray appeared to be considering what to say next. After some thought, he said, "I think this trip has been good for us. We've left all the distractions of the world behind. There is nothing to worry about here—no work, no school, no ferrying the kids from one event to the next, no schedules to keep, no bills to pay. We can just focus on each other."

It did feel like Ray and I had slipped right back into the routine of our relationship once we'd left home. Perhaps this trip was helping us to see each other through clear eyes again.

"Mom, Dad, this place looks good," Ty said, as we caught up with the boys.

"Great, let's order," Ray said, as we made our way to the counter.

After we ordered and took our seats under a fan, Ray asked, "What do you think things will look like when we get back home?"

Home was now literally half a world away and I didn't want to think about what I'd left behind—or what I'd be going back to. I wasn't even sure I wanted to go back at all.

Days of Travel: 33
Miles Logged: 13,016

HINDSIGHT

Singapore/Malaysia Border

Crossing into Malaysia from Singapore would mean we were truly on our own in the world without the support of a military base. The base in Singapore, although foreign, would be the last we'd encounter until we made our way across the entire continent of Asia, and eventually into western Europe. Even though we had made a point to get off base as soon as we could, there was always a hint of security knowing we could return and make our way home if we needed to. Now we would cross the border literally and figuratively into new territory.

"Let's go, let's go, let's go." I was trying to hustle everyone out of the hotel and into a taxi.

"Why are we in such a hurry?" Ty asked, loading his backpack into the trunk.

"Where are we going?" RJ added. He was great at going with the flow as long as he knew the plan.

I repeated the schedule for the day. "The ticket window opens at 7:00 a.m. If tickets sell out, we'll miss the connector train into Malaysia, which means we'll miss the next train to Kuala Lumpur, which means we'll have to spend another day in Singapore and do this all over again tomorrow." I counted the backpacks one last time and climbed into the backseat with the boys.

"We're going to Kuala Lumpur, RJ. A city in Malaysia," Ray answered calmly, turning to look at him.

"Another country?" RJ asked.

Ray nodded. "Yes. Another country."

The driver pulled up to the station minutes before the ticket office opened. We unloaded and got in line for commuter tickets to the Malaysia train station. Tickets in hand, our next stop was immigration. Walking down the corridor to get stamped out of Singapore, we encountered a long line of travelers doing the same thing. I had not factored in time for waiting in a queue.

I stood on tiptoes trying to see the front of the line. I could feel sweat pooling in every pore, my heart racing.

"We have plenty of time. Why do you fret so much?" Ray asked, leaning against the wall and breaking out his phone.

"There are so many steps and I don't want to mess up." We shuffled along, the line moving but not as fast as I wanted it to. "And I like to be early. This plan didn't leave much wiggle room." I looked at the line in front of us where no one else seemed to be feeling the same sense of urgency.

I had read the description of how to get from Singapore to Kuala Lumpur on a travel website dedicated to global train travel. Before 1965, all one had to do was catch a train in downtown Singapore. However, the process had increased in difficulty when Singapore gained independence from Malaysia. When the two countries separated, Malaysians retained ownership of the Singapore rail station, the railway, and the land it stood on. Because the Singapore government failed to gain control, the downtown station closed. Since that time, the only way to depart Singapore by train was to catch a shuttle train to Malaysia from a station thirteen miles north of the city, which you could only reach by taxi. While this description sounded straightforward, each step along the route contained several sub-steps, many of which could not be executed ahead of time, like buying commuter tickets or getting through passport control and immigration.

Ray tilted his head and looked at me over his glasses. "Trust yourself a bit. We all do." He nodded and stared at me until he made sure I was really hearing him. "If you've read it a hundred times, then you know we're doing all the right things. What's the worst that could happen? We spend one more night in Singapore?"

He was right, but I couldn't quite get to a point where I could turn off the questions zipping through my brain and my fear of messing things up. How do I know when the travel writer last made this journey? Who checked his instructions for accuracy? What if things had changed?

"I'd just like a little more time to adjust if we need to. And I worry about you guys, too," I added, looking at Tyler and RJ.

"Mom, we're fine. We can keep track of ourselves," Ty said.

I really hoped he was talking about keeping track of their belongings and keeping up with us on this trip and not anything more. I worried I'd checked out as a parent during The Glitch. There is so much growth in children in such a short span of time—mentally, physically, consciously—and I continued to feel as if I'd only been half present during those years. That perhaps I'd lost some vital connection to my boys.

"I know you can keep track of yourselves, but it's still my responsibility to make sure everyone has everything and stays together."

Given the circumstances, my boys had a lot to deal with at a young age and probably did more growing up than their peers, but I still wanted them to have a mother to look to when they were in need.

Finally, we were waved to the immigration booth and stamped out of Singapore. A few more twists and turns, down a corridor to another immigration stand, and we were stamped into Malaysia.

"That was easy," said RJ.

I looked at my boy, so like his father in his optimism. "We still have two more trains to catch. We're not quite done yet."

Getting through the first obstacle provided some relief. Timing for the initial ticketing and the immigration process was the most unpredictable piece we would face. Finding the right trains would be the easy part.

At least I had followed through on researching and making a hotel reservation in Kuala Lumpur before we left Singapore. Even if our day of travel went off track at some point (not literally, I prayed), we would end the day in a comfortable room away from any red-light district.

Standing in line and trying to will the line to move faster, I thought about Ray's question: *Why do you fret so much?* Ultimately the answer always came down to my desire to know what I was getting into and doing things right. I longed to have some command over my environment, but losing seven people in five short years left me grasping, trying to relieve the extreme discomfort, trying to regain my sense of self, anywhere I thought I could.

I nudged Ray and said, "I just want to make sure I am doing things right."

He looked at me with one eyebrow raised in question, having no idea I was answering a question meant to be rhetorical. "What are you talking about?"

"Why I fret so much. I just don't want to mess up." I rested my head on his shoulder for a moment, relieved a bit at having said the words out loud and given him a glimpse into my thought process.

"There's nothing in the world you can do that would mess things up for us," he said. Then, after a beat, he added, "Don't take that as a challenge, though."

I laughed and marveled again at how this man I married had the ability to infuse light into my darkness. "C'mon, let's go catch those trains."

Thankfully, after our ticket buying, immigration, and transferring from train to train, we made it out of Singapore and into Malaysia with relative ease. I plopped into my seat and stared out the window at the passing scenery. The seven-hour ride took us past palm and rubber tree plantations and small country stations. The clacking of the wheels and sway of the train car fell into a rhythm as we peeked through back doors into people's homes and got a glimpse of rural Malaysian life. Children in bare feet and threadbare clothing chased chickens and played with sticks. Men chopped down vegetation ever-threatening to swallow their property. Women washed and hung dingy clothes on outdoor lines. Everyone smiling, seemingly happy. Watching these people in five-second clips as we raced past, I could feel a tug toward happiness, like it was lurking just under the surface—unattainable, like a half-remembered dream, waiting for the right time to emerge.

Kuala Lumpur, Malaysia

As we approached Kuala Lumpur, small villages gave way to larger brick apartment buildings and then glass-encased skyscrapers, the slow pace of rural farm life replaced with the bustle of activity in a metropolis. I watched with fascination as the single track split into two, then four, and four again. The train pulled into a station lined with trains and platforms and clogged with people.

As we stepped onto the platform, I tapped Ray on the shoulder. "I have to stop at the bathroom before we find a taxi," I said, squirming a bit.

"Why didn't you just go on the train?" Ray asked.

"Uh, did you use the bathroom on the train?" I asked with wide eyes and raised eyebrows.

While the train had facilities, it was lacking in plumbing, allowing waste to drop straight from your body right onto the tracks below, along with any paraphernalia used to clean up afterward.

Ray laughed. "Yes, I noticed at the last station. I decided to go when the train was stopped. I looked out the window midstream and realized everyone at the station could see my head through the window and my pee falling onto the tracks!"

RJ laughed. "That's gross, Dad."

"Exactly what I was avoiding! I'll be right back." I pointed to the stick figure in a dress. Some signs needed no translation.

I walked into the first open stall and then right back out again. The toilet was missing. I walked along the row of stalls looking in each empty door, only to find none contained a western-style toilet.

When I walked out, Ray shot me a concerned look. "Everything okay? What took so long . . . or do I want to know?"

"Maybe I should have used the bathroom on the train," I said. "There were no toilets in there, only squatty potties."

RJ and Tyler both erupted in laughter.

"What's a squatty potty?" RJ asked, sending his brother into another fit.

"Let's just say you basically have to squat over a small hole in the floor and hope your aim is on point. There are ridged areas on which to place your feet so you don't slip, and when you're all done, you can either clean up using the hose or pray you have some tissue." The boys looked at me questioningly. "Which I did." They dissolved into giggles all over again. "And then you rinse it all down with a bucket of water from a trough at the back of the stall," I explained, as we walked through the station.

"That actually gives me some anxiety," Ray said.

"Now that would be one place I can see you using The Force," I said with a laugh. "There's the taxi stand." I pointed to a ticket window near the front of the station.

"No taxis now," grumbled the attendant as we approached.

"Why are there no taxis?" I asked, thinking I was being scammed.

"Riot," he replied. "Take city train."

"The train will take us into the city?" I chose to ignore the riot comment. His instructions weren't quite connecting for me.

"Monorail," he huffed, and pointed more emphatically toward another counter farther in the station.

We discovered it was Malaysia Day—a celebration of independence. But due to some groups feeling marginalized, many people marched in protest. Police were firing chemical-laced water cannons into the crowds to combat the riots that had erupted.

Maybe I should have been more concerned about heading into a city in the middle of this chaos, but strangely enough, this did not give me one bit of anxiety. Riots were something you see on TV, far away, dealing with issues you sympathize with but don't fully understand, not something that would affect us. I didn't even consider the riot might be taking place near the train station or in the streets near our hotel. Apparently, neither did Ray, because neither of us hesitated.

The Kuala Lumpur train station, *KL Sentral*, was not only the hub for all major train lines running through the country, the intercity train line, and the monorail line, but it also housed hotels, office towers, condominiums, and a six-story shopping mall buzzing with activity.

Covered from head to toe except for their faces, Muslim women were dressed in bright blouses of every color worn over flowing skirts. Matching headscarves were adorned with sparkling beads and sequins in intricate patterns. The men, too, were covered in shirts that reached their knees, draped over baggy pants. Though the men's attire stayed neutral in all shades of browns, blacks, and whites. Although I was not scandalously dressed in a spaghetti-strap tank top and capri pants, I could feel the glares from the crowds on every inch of bare flesh and knew I was not covered enough.

We wandered through the crowds, making our way from the train terminal to the monorail line on the opposite side of *KL Sentral*, passing through the heart of the shopping mall along the way. Being forced into taking the monorail turned out to be an opportunity. We discovered how easy the monorail system was to use in this sprawling city and we used it regularly during our stay.

We spotted the hotel from the train and checked in, only slightly worn out from the day's adventures. I moaned when I entered our chilled room, the air-conditioning and the view of the Petronas Towers from the picture window rewarding us for our perseverance. The towers were lit from ground floor to the eighty-eighth, making them visible through the haze, but it was apparent we would not be visiting the observatory on this trip. Our view of the cylindrical twin glass-and-steel skyscrapers connected by a public sky bridge and towering over the rest of the smaller skyscrapers in the downtown area would have to suffice. Even here, smoke from the fires in Indonesia cast a haze over the city and visibility was poor.

Our hotel was a step up from our red-light special in Singapore and I was thrilled to see cotton sheets. While the kids lounged in our room, Ray and I ended the evening with a beer at the rooftop café. We kicked back and relaxed, happy to have made it to our destination. As we chatted about options for the next day, our conversation was interrupted by the Islamic call to prayer broadcast via loudspeaker from a nearby mosque.

Available to believer and non-believer alike, the call to prayer is a summary of Islamic belief. With the many ethnic groups already fighting over marginalization, I wondered how those practicing Buddhism, Christianity, or Hinduism were affected by this transmission five times a day. Freedom of speech and religion were etched into my belief system. If my neighborhood church blasted their beliefs over loudspeakers five times a day, I couldn't help but think I'd be brainwashed in no time. When you hear the same message repeatedly, no matter what the message is, at some point it sticks.

I took another swig of beer and thought about how I'd beaten myself so far down taking others' words to heart and absorbed Mom's words so fully that I let her memory dictate my behavior.

Ray set his empty beer bottle down on the table. "Do you want another one?"

"No, I'm good. Let's head in, see what the kids are up to." I didn't feel the need to drown my feelings anymore. I'd kept my promise to Ray about exercising moderation when it came to drinking. Though I knew if I wasn't numbing the echo of my ghosts, I would have to deal with them head on at some point.

Publicly, Mom sang my praises to friends and family. But away from the eyes and ears of others, she tore me down. A few weeks after our Hawaii trip, I'd brought Mom her evening tea and meds, setting the tray down on her nightstand, careful not to spill the tea.

"Here you go, Mom." I breathed through my mouth to avoid the smell of decaying flesh seeping from the open wound on her leg.

Mom was no longer able to care for herself and was in her final weeks of life, her disease progressing and her demeanor deteriorating on a daily basis.

She looked around the room, searching for a clock. "Already? It can't possibly be time." She seemed confused and looked at me as if I were trying to trick her.

"It's seven o'clock. Time for the evening dose." I handed her a towel to soak up any drips.

She ignored the towel as she grabbed her phone and began swiping through apps and then photos and then contacts.

I tried to be patient, but knew she'd started down a never-ending path. "What are you looking for?" I asked.

Still flipping through screens, she barked, "What do you think I'm looking for? I have to find the sheet listing all the medication I'm supposed to take to make sure I'm not overdosing!"

This had become her routine. Four times a day, she'd try to find the picture of the sheet we'd created listing the correct dosage of each medicine. She'd examine each pill down to the shape and markings and compare it to the picture on her phone. After every doctor's appointment, we'd update the list of medications, double-check all pill boxes, and reload the sorter precisely to prevent any mis-dosages. This had become a necessity after I'd found Mom had inadvertently tripled her steroid dose. The cancer and subsequent radiation had destroyed part of her brain, making basic calculations impossible.

"Mom, we organized the pills together. They're correct." I hoped my voice conveyed calm. Inside I was anything but tranquil.

"There's so many pills. It seems like too many. And I don't like taking that huge one. It's hard to swallow." She curled her lip in disgust as she struggled to prop herself up.

I watched to ensure she swallowed the antibiotic. "If you don't, your leg could get reinfected. It's looking pretty bad." I knew by the putrid odor that the infection had already returned.

She took a drink and tossed her head back. "Oh, what do you know! You think you know everything. Looking down your nose like you're so much better than me, like I don't know anything. You're so uncaring when you speak to me. And you treat the rest of your family like that, too. I'm surprised Ray has put up with you this long. If I were him, I would have left you long ago."

I stood still, teeth gritted, eyes unblinking, and lungs barely expanding. Even if I believed with every fiber of my being this was only the medication talking or only the result of the brain damage caused by the cancer or radiation, I believed hidden somewhere in her words was a kernel of truth about how she saw me.

Her words continued to fill my head and expand but I didn't respond. Any reaction on my part would incite an argument I didn't have the energy to engage in.

"You speak to him like he's a child, just like you do with me. Like an infection matters at this point! They might as well cut my leg off. Don't you think I know I'm dying?"

I ignored the "dying" comment, trying instead to steer the conversation away from me and back to the medication.

"Mom, I don't speak to you like you're a child. It's not easy to go through this same routine four times a day and get you to take all the pills."

"Easy for who? You? Oh, poor little Lisa. I'm so sorry you have to make tea and bring me pills every day. Excuse me for being so difficult to deal with. How do you think I feel? Lying here in your house, all of my dignity stripped away, you and Ray whispering behind my back." Her voice rose as she worked herself up. "You're probably hoping I die tomorrow. Is that what you want? Me gone? You wouldn't have to do anything for me then. Just keep pulling the wool over Ray's eyes and giving those kids everything they want so they can grow up to be spoiled brats and treat you just like you're treating me."

It took all my strength to hold back my emotion and watch her swallow the rest of the pills. "Do you need anything else?" I asked, my voice cold, devoid of any sympathy.

"No. You can run away now." She brushed me away with the wave of a hand, dismissing me from the room.

The sensitive part of me wanted to fall to my knees and beg her forgiveness for everything I had done to wrong her. The hard part of me refused to give in to her rant. The two halves were ripping me apart.

I walked out of her room to find Ray waiting for me in the hall, looking at me with disbelief and empathy.

"I didn't realize it was that bad." He held his arms open.

The look of disgust on my mother's face as she reduced me to nothing would be the memory that stuck with me, camouflaging any happy memories I might have known. Only her scorn remained, seeming to follow me all the way across the world to Malaysia.

Even with Mom gone, the memory of her words continued to drive my actions. I was still striving to do things "right" so I wouldn't disappoint Ray or my boys. But no one in my family held the same lofty expectations, so why did I continue to strive for some imaginary ideal?

Aroused from sleep by the call to prayer just before 6:00 a.m., we set out to visit Batu Caves, the most popular Hindu shrine outside of India. Now confident in taking the monorail, we made two transfers and then took a short walk to the entrance of the shrine, which was flanked by hundreds of macaque monkeys—some scavenging for food on sidewalks and in dumpsters, others climbing buildings or swinging from statues, but all ready for an opportunity to steal food or shiny objects. Ray and I had read about the monkeys but opted not to tell the kids about them. Their excitement over encountering monkeys for the first time was our reward for secrecy.

"Mom, look!" RJ said, pointing at the monkey closest to us.

Ty scanned the tops of buildings. "They're all over the place,"

"Let's find something to feed them," Ray said with a mischievous grin.

"No way," I interrupted, before the boys caught on to the idea. "Look at that sign—No Feeding the Monkeys. They're wild animals." I backed away from the troop of animals, noticing several whose fur was falling out in places. And possibly rabid, I thought.

We continued to walk toward a hundred-and-forty-foot-tall statue of Lord Murugan, a Hindu deity, shining bright, completely covered in gold paint. The statue served as the guardian to a daunting staircase that rose up the limestone mountain and disappeared into the mouth of a colossal cave. After admiring Murugan, we climbed the two hundred and seventy-two stairs to a landing flanked on both sides by vendors selling souvenirs and cheap trinkets. Passing through the flea-market atmosphere, we entered the open-roof cave to visit the shrine, which itself was not impressive. The natural beauty of the cave was diminished by a worn gazebo constructed in the middle of the space. The structure was adorned with gods and holy animals, once painted in bright colors, now faded and peeling. The entire area felt run-down, dirty. Trash was scattered over the floor and spilled carelessly from trash cans. This holy location looked like a tornado had swept through it, leaving garbage and debris in its path. I thought for a moment about why those who worship in this holy space would ignore the dirty conditions. And, then I realized, perhaps that was only my interpretation of the *right* way. Perhaps those who worshipped here were focused not so much on the exterior of the shrine as much as the place itself and what it represented.

After touring the cave, we ended the day with a visit to the open-air Chinese Chow Kit Market located in the streets right outside our hotel. As we searched for a place to eat, Ty had his first superstar moment. While handsome in his own right, with thick, sandy-brown hair and sparkling hazel eyes, Tyler attracted special attention in Asian countries by towering over everyone. As we passed by a clothing stall, a girl called out,

"Boy, boy, I want one picture with you. Can I take one picture with you?" Ty agreed, and she had her friend take the photo. The girls giggled and said he looked like Justin Bieber. He was a bit embarrassed but flattered as much as a teenage boy can be. While this small gesture was endearing, we would all soon tire of being the center of attention.

As we continued through the market, we were bombarded by vendors trying to lead us to their stalls and sell us every manner of trinket and tour. If we paused even for a moment to have a conversation or figure out directions, vendors seized the opportunity. We needed to find a way to have a discussion without distraction.

"All right, everyone, circle up!" I said, as we were trying to decide where to eat.

"What?" RJ asked, unsure of what I wanted.

I grabbed one of RJ's arms and one of Tyler's pulling, them close. "Now, Ray, close the circle."

"It's really more of a square, Mom," Tyler said.

"Fine, then, square up," I said. "We just have to block the outside world for a few seconds."

With our family knotted together, shoulder to shoulder, backs facing the outside, we sent a clear message that we did not want to be intruded upon. No outside influence could penetrate our family bond.

"Okay, where to for dinner?" Ray asked.

"Let's go to that first place we saw outside the hotel. That looked good," Tyler said.

I looked from face to face in our square and felt my heart opening in that moment. These were the faces most important in my life. None of them cared if I made mistakes in our travel plans. None of them expected perfection. None of them would have seen a setback at the border as anything more than just that, a setback, a temporary alteration of our plans. Not as an imperfection in my character that needed to be remedied.

I smiled. "All agreed?" I asked.

With nods all around, we broke our formation and set off for dinner.

"Square up? Where'd you come up with that?" Ray asked.

"I actually said 'circle,' Tyler changed it to 'square,'" I said.

"I like it!"

I didn't know if the sentiment would stick, but I felt secure in my place as one side of our family square.

Cameron Highlands

After some research, we decided to visit Cameron Highlands because of its location in the hills of Malaysia, where the average daily temperature drops significantly. During the day, it seldom gets above seventy-two degrees, and at night, rarely drops below forty-eight degrees. After more than a month of travel in tropical climates, we were ready to cool off.

Filled with self-assurance at having successfully navigated around Kuala Lumpur, Ray and I had a plan to get us to our next destination—catch a train to the small town of Ipoh, then transfer to a bus to take us into the highlands. We made it to the train station with plenty of time to spare, only to find that tickets for the morning train were sold out. Reminding myself to take things one step at a time, I asked if there was another way to get to Ipoh that morning. Directed to the bus station, we discovered all morning bus tickets to Ipoh were also sold out. Rather than weigh our options at this point and look for a different route, we made a rushed decision to continue down the path we had started and purchased tickets for the 3:00 p.m. bus to Ipoh.

We sat at the bus station, helping the boys with homework and watching movies on the Internet until it was time to leave. At three o'clock, we boarded the bus and, two hours later, we arrived in Ipoh and took a taxi for the remainder of the journey, approximately fifty-six miles with an elevation gain of four thousand feet. The taxi ride was a nausea-inducing, two-hour drive through winding roads filled with traffic jams.

When we finally arrived and checked in to a lovely hotel in the Cameron Highlands, we encountered an issue with the electricity in our room, and the manager had to come up to help us. While he was working on the power, he asked us about our trip. We told him about our adventure of taking the bus to Ipoh and then a taxi to Cameron Highlands.

"Why didn't you just take a bus from Kuala Lumpur directly to Cameron Highlands?" the manager asked, as if that were the most obvious choice.

A bus ride from Kuala Lumpur to Cameron Highlands would have taken us three and a half hours in total. Instead, we spent almost twelve hours trying to get from one place to the next. Ray and I looked at each other, dumbfounded. We'd made so many mistakes on this leg—from not buying tickets early to not thinking things through at the bus station. We could have saved hours of time (not to mention quite a few dollars) by stepping back for a minute and reevaluating. Apparently, The Force could be relied upon to a certain extent, but also required some human intervention and critical thinking from time to time.

While the locals were clad in mittens and scarves, I was comfortable in shorts and a T-shirt for the first time in weeks, in temperatures similar to our hometown of Bellingham on a warm summer night. We were gawked at once again walking around in our summer clothing eating ice cream.

The Cameron Highlands are well-known for two major crops—strawberries and tea. During our short stay in town, we set out to find both. We hired a driver for a few hours and went straight to breakfast at a strawberry farm. I had a strawberry muffin, strawberry pudding with fresh strawberries, vanilla ice cream (just for fun), and strawberry coffee—really a lot better tasting than it sounds. The flavors reminded me of Strawberry Shortcake cereal, a favorite of mine growing up. Ray, RJ, and Tyler had strawberry waffles or pancakes topped with ice cream and fresh strawberries, and an accompanying strawberry drink. Our driver would tell us later that diabetes was a huge problem in Malaysia.

"We should eat breakfast here every day," RJ commented. Tyler agreed.

I hadn't given much thought to our adopted travel diet, typically either eggs seasoned with soy sauce on a small baguette or noodle soup, but I had to admit sweet pink everything for breakfast was a nice change. Although I still longed for a plain black cup of coffee, rather than the sickly sweet, condensed milk with a splash of coffee I found most often.

After our strawberry breakfast, our driver took us to visit a tea plantation. In a lifetime of drinking tea, I'd never considered where tea came from or how it was grown. The hillside was covered in short, round bushes as far as I could see. I could taste it in air, the strong scent of sun-warmed tea flooding in through the open window. If such a small glimpse could give me a whole new understanding of something, I wondered how much RJ and Tyler were learning on this trip, even in the smallest of details they might not even realize. I thought again of how this would not have been possible had I turned around at the outset, and I felt some satisfaction in knowing we were all learning on this adventure.

After our day of touring the highlands, our driver returned us to our hotel. Before heading to the hotel dining room for dinner, we stopped at the front desk to inquire about the best way to get to our next destination. Apparently, even Ray was becoming aware of when The Force needed some added human input.

The manager waved us to the front desk. "How can I help you?" he asked.

"We were wondering if you could tell us where we need to catch the bus tomorrow. We're hoping to get to George Town on the island of Penang."

"Ah, I know the driver. I'll call and have him stop here on his way out of town in the morning. I will arrange for a taxi to take you from the bus depot to Penang. Be ready by nine," he replied. And, without hesitation, shooed us off to dinner and picked up the phone to make the arrangements.

"Great. See you in the morning," I said. Ray and I walked away from the front desk a little shocked at the manager's thoughtfulness.

"Do you think he does that for everyone?" I asked, as we made our way to the restaurant in the hotel.

"Maybe he feels sorry for us," Ray answered.

Either way, I was happy to have someone else make arrangements to get us to our next destination. I was getting better at using The Force, but letting someone with more knowledge do the planning for once was nice. I was a little worried about where we might end up the next day, but decided wherever it might be, I'd deal with it when we got there.

George Town, Penang Island

Thanks to the hotel manager, a taxi waited at the bus depot to take us over the nearly nine-mile-long bridge to the island of Penang.

While George Town is a large metropolitan city of nearly a million people, we chose to stay in the historical district famed for its prominent street art and mix of colonial and Asian architecture.

As soon as we reached our hotel, I called out to the boys on their way to their room, "Hang on guys, let's square up for a minute."

"Seriously, Mom? You're going to use that now?" Tyler rolled his eyes.

"Yes. I like it," I said. "Let's make a plan for what we want to see in George Town. Maybe we can each pick something."

"What are our choices?" RJ asked.

"Well, there's Penang Hill, where we can visit Monkey Cup Garden, There's a Buddhist shrine somewhere near there, too. We can do a tour of old town, which has a lot of street art . . ." I looked at the boys to see if any of the options piqued their interest.

"It all sounds kind of boring, Mom," Tyler said.

RJ added, "Monkeys sound fun."

I didn't want to tell RJ right then that Monkey Cup Garden was full of plants, not monkeys.

"I think we should do all of it," Ray said, trying to amp up the boys' enthusiasm.

After we were settled, Ray led us on a self-guided walking tour through old town, including Chinatown and Little India. Colorful murals decorated practically every building. Some were as small as a piece of paper, while others dominated the entire side of a building, incorporating the building features, such as windows and doors, into the piece. We found wrought-iron sculptures of cartoon characters at major intersections, which provided a historical context to the name of the street or the area of town.

By the early evening, the heat had again sapped our energy and we were all soaked with sweat. We found a small restaurant with eight tables where we could write on the walls and add our own little piece of art to the city. Every inch of every wall, and even the ceiling, was covered with names and sketches in every color of Sharpie imaginable.

I watched the boys write their names on the wall and then asked, "Still think today was boring?"

"No, it was actually pretty fun," RJ said.

Tyler nodded in agreement.

The next morning, we took a funicular train—a train that moves vertically up a slope using a cable-and-pulley system—to the top of Penang Hill. We had finally traveled far enough north that the smoke from fires in Indonesia had dissipated somewhat. Once at the top of the hill, we had a clear view across the strait between the island of Penang and mainland Malaysia. While the air still held a slight haze, I could see blue sky. I thought back to the blessing in Singapore and tried to hold the song in my heart, focus on clearing away my own clouds.

We walked along a paved road at the top of Penang Hill for a couple of miles to reach Monkey Cup Garden.

"Where are the monkeys?" RJ asked when we reached the entrance.

"Sorry, RJ, this is a garden for the Monkey Cup plant," I said. He scrunched his face, clearly less enthused about plants.

Monkey cup is the common name for *Nepenthes*, a tropical pitcher plant, of which the Monkey Cup Garden had practically every known variety. The garden was run by an energetic woman. Although her wrinkled skin and gray, thinning hair suggested she was quite old, the sparkle in her eye and enthusiasm of her greeting said otherwise. She welcomed us in, gave us a quick overview of the gardens, and sent us on a self-guided tour.

"Why is it called Monkey Cup if there aren't any monkeys?" RJ asked, still disappointed by not finding any monkeys.

"It's a nickname because the plants act as a pitcher to collect water," I started. The boys both began to smirk, and I wondered what I'd said that was so funny. "In the jungle, monkeys use the plants as a cup and drink the collected water."

The boys were now in full laughter. I glanced behind me to see Ray acting like a monkey and demonstrating how one might get a drink from the plant.

After our walk through the garden, the woman offered refreshments at a small stone table. The boys opted for sodas, but my eyes locked on a familiar octagonal aluminum pot, and I knew this Italian contraption could brew up a perfect espresso in under five minutes. The rich velvety brew quenched my desire for coffee and gave me a little jolt of caffeine as a bonus.

As we sat and sipped our drinks, I watched the woman repeat her greeting with every person who walked in, treating each like a favorite neighbor.

Another guide at the garden approached us with his hand outstretched, a sleek black scorpion resting on his palm.

"Do you want to hold it?" he asked.

"Is it safe?" Ray asked, a question that continued to come up with some regularity.

"Yes. This scorpion has big claws, small stinger. A sting would feel like a bee. Scorpions with small claws and large stingers, those are the poisonous ones," he explained.

I had an instant urge to scream "no!" The number of issues that I conjured related to holding a scorpion almost overwhelmed me. But instead of letting my worries override the situation, I decided to trust the guide and give Ray and the boys a chance to make their own choice. They, too, needed to learn to trust their decisions.

Ray looked at the man as if trying to judge the truth of his story, but in the end agreed to hold the scorpion. The man showed Ray how to hold his hand—palm facing the ground—and then he placed the scorpion on the back of Ray's hand. Ray moved his hand near his face to get a closer look.

"How about you boys?" The guide nodded toward the boys.

Encouraged by Ray, Tyler also agreed to hold the scorpion, but RJ was not up for this adventure. He was fascinated by the scorpion but wanted to keep a safe distance.

"How about on your head?" the guide asked. "Just like this." He took the scorpion from Ray and placed it on his own head.

Tyler looked at me. "On my head?"

I shrugged, giving him permission to decide for himself.

"Yes, will make a good picture." The guide gave him a wink.

"Okay," Ty said, with only the slightest hesitation.

The guide placed the scorpion on Ty's head, and we snapped a few pictures, Tyler grinning from ear to ear, almost disbelieving he had a giant black scorpion the length of his hand on top of his head. I couldn't quite believe it, either.

We left the garden, all of us abuzz from the adrenaline rush of holding a scorpion, or possibly the dose of caffeine.

"Where to next?" Tyler asked. I could tell he was enjoying today's adventure.

"I want to see the Buddhist statue," I said.

When no one put up an argument, we took a bus to visit the Kek Lok Si Temple, which claimed to be the largest Buddhist temple in Southeast Asia. Due to its location atop a steep hill, we were again faced with a daunting number of stairs to climb. We wound up and up the covered circular walkway lined with stalls selling everything from T-shirts to Buddha ashtrays. Although I was disappointed that the view of the city was covered by the T-shirts and cloths strung between the open pillars, I began to see the wisdom of the vendor stalls all along the winding stairway— the shops gave me something to look at when I needed a rest from my climb.

We continued up the winding stone stairway to a landing where a short funicular train carried us up the last stretch of the hill. Any option to climb the rest of the way was out of the question. The heat and humidity taxed our energy. We emerged to see a ninety-nine-foot bronze statue of Kuan Yin, the Goddess of Mercy, housed under an octagonal pavilion with ornately carved stone pillars supporting the roof.

Ray and the boys wandered around the area getting a look at the many statues surrounding Kuan Yin. I stood in front of this peaceful woman, shielding my eyes from the midday sun, and read the description: *This statue of Kuan Yin shows her right arm extended below her waist, palm facing upward, representing the granting of wishes to those who welcome the teaching of Buddhism. Her left arm is raised to shoulder level with thumb and middle finger touching, symbolizing great compassion.*

I stumbled on the last word—compassion, a trait my mom often claimed I lacked. Could it be true I had no compassion for my mother? I trailed behind Ray and the boys as we wandered through the gardens and temples, thinking about how Mom's story was much like my own. I tried to put myself in her place. She may not have had to deal with death as often, but she certainly had to deal with loss—her mother to illness, her father to alcohol, her loves to divorce, Zack to drugs.

I did have compassion for all the hardship she'd endured. There was a time as a young girl that I even looked up to Mom. But as time went on, the weight of the years, her failed marriages and relationships, and her own grief pulled her down and broke her spirit. As Zack's path took a negative turn, so did Mom's. Her days were clouded with depression and she sunk into a blackness I couldn't grasp. Her failure to be a parent to Zack was incomprehensible to me. I couldn't understand why she failed to fight, and I built a wall between us, plugging up every crack and crevice where compassion might seep through. Perhaps I thought withholding my affection would force her to act. Only looking back now could I see Mom's whole picture and where I took a wrong turn in shutting her out of my inner life. Only in hindsight could I see we had both been suffering.

Wanting to get a last look at Kuan Yin, I circled back and gazed up at her peaceful face. The whole adventure in Malaysia had been one big lesson in hindsight. I'd struggled for years to do things "right," but here in Malaysia, I learned there was no such thing. I didn't use the bathroom on the train, but learned how to use a squatty potty; we couldn't get a taxi to our hotel in Kuala Lumpur, but learned how to use the monorail; we rushed into a decision on getting to Cameron Highlands, but learned to reevaluate when our plans went off track—each mistake contributing to my knowledge and understanding of the world. There were actions and consequences. Hopefully, you learn from mistakes and choose a different action the next time you're faced with the same situation. The key was surrounding yourself with people who would forgive your mistakes and build you up as you faced the next set of challenges.

Holding the gaze of the Goddess of Mercy, I understood that part of clearing the negativity was discovering the road-blocks in the way and working to clear them. And, I made a choice. I offered myself compassion.

Days of Travel: 42
Miles Logged: 14,228

DAUGHTERS OF WAR

Hanoi, Vietnam

I was thirteen years old when the movie *Platoon* came out. My dad was stunned by the reality of the film, saying it was the only movie he'd seen that conveyed the mental and emotional realities of the Vietnam War. He took me to see it so I would understand what he'd been through. As the credits rolled and the house lights came up, Dad sat with tears streaming down his cheeks. He told me he felt as if he were watching his own story replayed right before his eyes. At thirteen, I couldn't comprehend the scope of what the war had meant for my father, but from that day, I never blamed him for being little more than a passing figure in and out of my life. I blamed Vietnam. I would return to this movie again and again to get to know him and understand his absence in my life.

Other than the events depicted in a two-hour film, I knew little about Dad's history or Vietnam itself, and I was nervous about going there. Born during the latter part of the Vietnam War, I understood next to nothing about this distant country other than what I'd heard growing up, none of which was good. The word "Nam" seemed to carry a tremendous weight, often inciting feelings of sorrow, regret, and revulsion.

"I just worry about how the people will feel about us," I said to Ray. "I imagine a country full of angry people who will despise us simply for being American."

Around the same time, we started dreaming of a trip around the world, Ray spent six weeks on the USNS Mercy—a thousand bed Navy hospital ship—as part of the 2010 Pacific Partnership training mission. The Mercy visited Vietnam, Cambodia, Indonesia, and Timor-Leste, treated 109,754 patients, and performed 1,580 surgeries on this humanitarian mission. Ray spent his time providing dental care in remote villages in Vietnam and Cambodia and fell in love with the countries. His experience of Vietnam contrasted with my vision of a country that had stolen my father from me, and of which, even these many years later, I was still wary of.

"I was hesitant before I actually went there," Ray said. "But I enjoyed my time there so much—the food, the people, the cities. I really want you and the boys to enjoy that same experience. Trust me. You'll see."

Landing in Hanoi, four countries into our trip, we had established a new-country routine. With hotel arrangements made in advance and Ray's study of cultural norms before we arrived, The Force was strong with our family. After clearing customs—the easiest customs process thus far on the trip—we hit an ATM before even stepping foot outside the airport. Not only were we armed with information and local currency, but suddenly, with an exchange rate of twenty-two thousand Vietnamese dong to one United States dollar, our bank account showed we were millionaires!

I'd booked a hotel in the Old Quarter, a district of Hanoi that has existed since imperial times and centrally located among the tourist attractions, which also meant more tourists and businesses who catered to tourists. The streets were lined with vendor after vendor selling everything from kitchen utensils to knockoff brand clothing. Restaurants abounded and we were hungry.

In single file, we sidestepped our way through a sea of people. Restaurant patrons paused their slurping of noodles and looked up at us from their low plastic stools and tables. At this point we were used to being stared at, but we felt even more daunted by the sheer number of people in the streets and the hundreds of eyes turned in our direction. Walking behind Tyler, I could feel his resistance growing.

"Let's stop for a minute." I wanted to look at him, gauge how he was coping with all the people. "Ty, what's going on?"

Ty wrinkled his nose. "Can't we find somewhere else, with fewer people?"

"Why?" Ray asked.

"I don't like feeling like the center of attention. Everyone is staring at me and I feel totally out of place," he said.

I could tell by his shrinking demeanor that Ty felt especially uncomfortable, his lanky frame an anomaly in a country where 5'1" was the average for males. I was not completely at ease, either. Vietnam was still an unknown.

After some searching, we found a less conspicuous restaurant on the second floor of a building with standard-size tables and chairs. Being above the street, watching the crowds from our table on the balcony, Tyler didn't feel so exposed, and we all relaxed as we experimented with chopsticks and scarfed down savory dishes of noodles and rice with names we could not pronounce.

Setting out the next morning to explore Vietnam's turbulent past, we were like children learning how to function in the world. Figuring out how to eat with chopsticks had been easy compared to learning how to cross the street.

Following our map, we found ourselves on a busy motorway with no discernible traffic light or crosswalk. The six-lane road was filled with hundreds of motorcycles racing every which way, many carrying huge loads—as many as five passengers, ladders, sometimes even a big-screen TV or a jumble of bamboo crates loaded with chickens. Few drivers wore helmets, opting for the traditional Vietnamese farmer's conical hat.

"How do we get across?" RJ asked, looking left and right at the throng of motorcycles zipping in both directions.

"I read about this online," Ray started. "You just have to wait for an opening, step off the curb, and walk at a steady pace until you're across."

Ray's declaration did not fill me with ease. "You read about it online?" I asked.

"Dad, that doesn't sound safe," Tyler added.

Ray continued to focus on the traffic, watching for an opening, "Drivers will go around us if we keep a steady pace."

RJ took hold of the back of Ray's shirt, pulling him back from the edge of the sidewalk. "It's too dangerous, Dad."

"We'll be fine. Just remember to keep walking," Ray assured him. "Oh, and don't look a driver in the eye."

"What the hell does that have to do with crossing the street?" I yelled over the noise of the traffic.

"I don't know. I read something about potentially sending the wrong message about who has the right of way," he answered offhandedly.

Ty rolled his eyes. "You just made that up, didn't you?"

Ray ignored his question. "Better if we all go at once. Safety in numbers."

"This doesn't sound promising," I said.

"Okay, there's an opening!" Ray pointed. "And . . . go!"

We stayed together in a clump and walked at a steady pace across the street. I could feel the sputter of exhaust on my bare legs as the motorcycles darted around us, much too close for my comfort, but none running directly into us.

Once on the sidewalk, Ray turned to all of us with a triumphant grin. "See? You just have to trust the process."

I watched locals and realized that maybe Ray had figured something out in his research, since all the other pedestrians were following the same process—walk with a constant gait and no hesitation, let the motorcycles go around you, and don't look anyone in the eye.

A few more quick crossings and we arrived at the Hoa Lo Prison, a name loosely translated as "Hell Hole" and more commonly known to Americans as the "Hanoi Hilton," a POW camp during the Vietnam War. While Ray and I had decided early in our planning that museums would be a good way to introduce world history to the boys. I also hoped a visit to Dad's past might add to my understanding of him.

Dad was an every-other-weekend parent, provided he lived in the same town, or the same state, or didn't have to work, or he didn't have a girlfriend, or if he was sober. And sometimes, even if he wasn't. When Dad did show up, my world was complete. Maybe it was the lack of time together that made each visit so special. I cherished weekends with Dad. Together, we had a comfortable routine. He'd pick me up and first we'd visit my grandparents. Next, we'd go to his apartment where he'd cook dinner—always Shake 'N Bake Barbeque chicken and herb and butter Rice-A-Roni. He'd pour us each a glass of neon red Hawaiian Punch that mirrored the hand-me-down, red Formica table and red vinyl chairs in his closet-sized kitchen. Dinner was followed by a game of cribbage where Dad taught me how to be a champion. As the night wound to a close, Dad would turn on a movie and make his way to a back room once my attention was diverted. He'd return to the sofa trailed by a pungent, earthy odor I was too young to identify.

His unpredictable visits caused my relationship with my dad to be one defined by disappointment. Often, with my overnight bag packed, I'd sit on the front steps of my house waiting for his car to turn the corner, willing the phone to remain silent. Sometimes he was responsible enough to call and tell Mom he wasn't coming for me; sometimes, I waited for hours before she could coax me back into the house. Eventually, I stopped waiting for him.

Once I graduated from high school and made my way to Bellingham, our conversations became infrequent and meetings even rarer. I'd always try to see him when I returned to Butte, but finding him was not guaranteed. When my boys were four and five, Dad showed up at a family picnic and met his grandchildren for the first time. In a rare lucid moment, he promised to join me the next morning for coffee before we returned to Bellingham. He played with RJ and Tyler and promised to bring them boxes of Matchbox cars he'd been saving for them. Eager to believe that perhaps my children could be the bridge back to a relationship with him, I let myself believe it was true. But the next morning, I found myself by the window waiting for his car to round the corner, once again willing the phone not to ring.

When he was more than an hour overdue, Ray laid a hand on my arm and said, "Lisa, we can't wait any longer. He's not coming."

My heart broke all over again, the familiar disappointment rising in my throat. But breaking promises to my kids was an offense I wouldn't tolerate. Although RJ and Tyler barely noticed his absence, I made a silent promise to never let them experience the same disappointment all too familiar to me. I didn't know that none of us would ever see him again.

Three years later, when Ray and I returned to Butte for Dad's funeral and to sort through the remains of his life, we found two shoe boxes filled with Matchbox cars, one labeled "RJ" and the other "Tyler." On top of the boxes we found road maps of Washington with Bellingham circled repeatedly in the upper left-hand corner. Perhaps he longed to be more than just a shadow in our lives. Somehow, that made his passing even harder.

Ray and the boys wandered off to explore the museum's earlier history as a French prison, while I was drawn to the Vietnam War era. As I walked through the quiet rooms showcasing the propaganda broadcast by the prison during the war—pictures of American pilots sharing Christmas dinner, playing basketball and having a grand time as they waited to be released—my resentment mixed with longing.

Ray caught up with me looking at the pictures of American POWs smiling over a turkey dinner.

"Do you remember that night after the funeral? My aunts and uncles recounting Dad's stories about the war?" I asked.

"Yep, that was rough."

"His stories never included a turkey. These photos are bullshit," I said. "And none of these pictures show what it was like fighting in the jungles."

Dad had told me only a single story of his time in the jungle, but after he died, I heard more than I was prepared for. On the evening of his funeral, a crowd of family and friends gathered at my grandma's house to send Dad off with a toast and a good old-fashioned Irish wake. As the evening wore on, liquor loosened tongues, and Ray and I sat back and listened to my aunts and uncles tell stories about their brother, and, inevitably, about the war.

Dad's oldest sister, Lee, was the first to bring up Vietnam. "I remember how mad I was that Bob wanted to enlist. I was so anti-war that I was just appalled when he said he wanted to shoot *gooks*." She swirled the wine in her glass, the blush of the rosé matching her cheeks. "He came to visit me in California one time when he was on leave and I noticed he'd changed. He slept in a hammock, preferring it to a bed. Over dinner, he talked about how horrible it was there."

She took a deep breath, her distress evident. Dad had shown her pictures of dead men lying on the ground because his superiors encouraged the soldiers to take pictures of their kills. He was upset he was made to do that, but it was expected. Lee placed her wine glass on the table and lit a cigarette, inhaling deeply. "When the boys over there were not in battle, they smoked dope and did all kinds of drugs in their tents. The brass knew what was going on, but they turned their backs. It's easy to see how that could mess with your head." She blew a cloud of smoke into the night air and took another sip of wine.

"I think Bob only told you the tame parts, Lee. The stories he told me were much worse," my Uncle Dan added. His face was concealed by a baseball cap and a thick, bushy beard, but his eyes said he was missing his older brother. Although normally quiet in social situations, a few drinks gave him the courage to voice the painful memories he'd been keeping to himself. "He told me it was the women and children that messed with his head. His superiors had ordered him to kill kids, and he talked about the raping and killing of women, too. I'm not sure he was a party to it, but he witnessed it at the very least."

Lee put her cigarette out in the ashtray and refilled her wine glass. "I'm glad he never told me that part of the story. I always knew the war had a tremendous impact on him, but I never suspected anything like that."

Back at the prison, I pointed at the picture of the turkey dinner and said to Ray, "My dad was never a POW, but I'm quite sure if this had been the Vietnam he'd experienced, I'd still have a dad. Did Americans know what conditions in Vietnam were really like?"

"I don't know. That was before my time, too. But remember, these photos are highlighting the propaganda that was released. The Vietnamese wanted Americans back home to believe that the POWs were being treated well," Ray answered.

I wondered what my mom had known of Dad's experiences in the war. Was she led to believe he was having turkey dinners and playing basketball? Could she have thought he'd return to the United States the same man he was when he left? Did she experience his night terrors or anxieties before deciding to have a baby with him? Or did she think having a baby would cure him? Did he feel the same?

I ached at my father's inability to reintegrate, at my mother's naivete, and their shared inability to conquer fears and heal their damaged selves.

"I think I'm ready to go," I said.

I left the museum not understanding anything more about my father.

Ha Long Bay

The next morning, the four of us stood on the narrow street in front of our hotel waiting for a van to pick us up and drive us to Ha Long Bay, an area with nearly two thousand limestone islands off the northern coast of Vietnam. The legend of Ha Long Bay—translated as "Where the Dragon Descends to the Sea"—tells of a dragon's force tearing up the Earth, the islands the only remnants of the destruction.

After listening to my description of the area, RJ asked, "Where are we staying?"

I smiled, knowing he'd be as excited about our accommodations for the night as I was. "We're going to stay on a boat and explore the islands for a couple days."

"Oh, cool!"

When the van pulled up, Ray opened the side doors and ushered us all into the vehicle.

The four-hour bus ride from Hanoi to Ha Long Bay proved to be the most perilous, nerve-wracking ride I'd ever been on. Speed limits and lane divisions were more suggestion than rule. Each time our driver attempted to pass a vehicle, I squeezed my eyes shut and clung to the arm rest, positive we were about to die in a fiery explosion. But no collision occurred. It seemed drivers had the same code as pedestrians—consistent speed, no hesitation, no direct visual contact.

When we arrived at the harbor, our tour guide, Cong, a young man of twenty-three who looked more like seventeen, led our group of ten to a double-decker boat. We were introduced to the captain and crew and given a tour. The main deck housed the kitchen and dining area, while the upper deck held a platform with deck chairs and loungers where one could relax in the sun. Finally, we were shown to our rooms below deck, each containing two single beds and a small bathroom behind a door we had to turn sideways to fit through. After dropping off our backpacks, we returned to the upper deck and stood along the rail to get a better view of the jagged limestone pillars jutting out of the water, one after another. The stresses of the road faded. I had to give Ray credit—the serenity of this place was the elixir my soul craved.

After a three-hour journey amid thousands of isles, the boat anchored and we boarded two-person kayaks. We paddled through a floating fishing village nestled in a quiet cove, made our way to a large island to explore caves, and ended the day with a swim off the boat in the warm waters of the South China Sea. While Ray and Tyler opted to jump the fifteen feet from the deck of the boat to the water below, RJ and I, along with several other passengers, opted for caution and took the ladder. I was surprised at the rush of water, the current pulling me away from the boat. I looked at the others and could see that we were all swimming hard to stay near the boat. I was thankful in that moment for the hours of swim lessons I'd sat through with my boys. It only took a few minutes before we were tired from the constant paddling the current demanded and we queued for the ladder.

After our evening swim, we sat with the other passengers on the main deck, sipping beers and enjoying the warm evening air. As we dried off, Cong—his starched white shirt never showing a wrinkle in this tropical climate—entertained us with stories about Vietnam and its people and encouraged a question-and-answer exchange. As he pushed his thick-rimmed glasses up the non-existent bridge of his nose, he said, "The difference between Americans and Vietnamese is that Americans kiss outside and pee inside, while Vietnamese pee outside and kiss inside." We all laughed. We'd seen our fair share of men peeing on the side of the road.

As the sun dipped below the craggy limestone isles, the conversation turned to the upcoming elections in Vietnam. We'd all noticed increased security patrols in the streets, purportedly reducing the risk of riots. Wanting to get a young person's perspective, I asked Cong about his thoughts on the elections. Some part of me longed to confirm my political views were more similar than different from the Vietnamese.

"I don't really have an opinion," he replied.

Surprised by his answer, I followed up with, "Are you going to vote?"

"No, I don't think my vote will make a difference. We get to vote, but the Communist party picks who is on the ballot. I'm happy to go along with whatever the majority decides."

"How do you feel about the Vietnam War?" Ray asked, glancing at Cong and then in my direction. "Do the Vietnamese harbor any resentment toward Americans and their involvement in the war?"

"No. The young people of Vietnam don't even think about it. That was our grandfathers' war. Not ours. We love Americans," Cong answered with enthusiasm.

His grandfather's war; my father's war. And in many ways, my war. Even though Dad was dead and the war over for nearly forty years, I was still clinging to all I'd heard about how this place had ruined him. My father had come home a changed man, unable to reintegrate into society. I lost my father to his demons. How did Cong, who lived right here, escape the same fate?

I drifted out of the discussion, trying to reconcile the conversation in my head. I was surprised at Cong's answer, but after some thought, I understood there might be several reasons he was not bound to the same mindset as me. While I thought of Vietnam only in how it destroyed my father and other veterans, the country had been subject to invasion by the French, Japanese, British, and Chinese, as well as by Americans. Well after the Vietnam War ended, China attacked Vietnam, and the threat of war with China loomed as a real possibility to this day. The Vietnamese consumed American movies, music, and fast food, just like many other nations. And maybe most important to the equation, Vietnam won the war, perhaps making magnanimity easier.

Da Nang

After our brief time in Hanoi and Ha Long Bay, we traveled by overnight train five hundred miles south to Da Nang where Ray was scheduled to work with orphans and disabled children at East Meets West Dental Center. We arrived October 2, seven weeks after leaving the United States.

Located at about the midpoint of the Vietnam coast at the mouth of the Han River, Da Nang is an important port city, but not a typical stop for tourists. While it is known for its sandy beaches and history as a French colonial port, tourists opt to visit the Ba Na Hill station and resort thirty miles to the west or the lantern-lit city of Hoi An, thirty miles to the south. We would not be spending a lot of time doing touristy things here as there weren't a lot of touristy things to do. Even the Lonely Planet guide claims that one day in Da Nang is sufficient for most people. While Ray was off doing his part to make the world a better place, I hoped to get the boys through a good amount of schoolwork. Although we had no formal school itinerary to follow, I wanted to make sure the boys learned at least a little something as we traveled.

Since foreign visitors in Da Nang were rare, few locals spoke English and businesses did not cater to an international crowd. No English translations meant we had a hard time the first few days trying to figure out what to order in restaurants. The point-and-nod method didn't always work out as we had expected. On our second night, we walked around the corner from the hotel and tried to sit at an outdoor café and order. No one working or eating at the restaurant spoke English, and there were no menus. In order to eat, we had to know both what we wanted and how to say it in Vietnamese. The best we could do was order beer (*bia* in Vietnamese) and soda. We ended up eating grilled cheese sandwiches ordered from room service at our hotel. But cheese in Vietnam is not like any cheese you would find in America. Its texture is slimy, and reminiscent, in both taste and texture, of orange Play-Doh. Thankfully, help was on the way. Our friends Lee and Snow flew from their home in Ho Chi Minh City to visit for the weekend.

I first met Lee when I moved to Bellingham from Butte. While he was quite a bit older than me, Lee and I became friends through our shared love of volleyball. When Ray came into my life, Lee quickly made friends with him, too, and they often enjoyed debating the topic of the day. At some point, Lee visited Vietnam to come to terms with his own part in the Vietnam War. During one of his visits, as he sat reading in a coffee shop, he was captivated by the independence of a young blind woman, deftly navigating her coffee preparation with only one hand. When he finished his coffee, he got up to leave, but was pulled back by an urge to speak to this young woman. Despite their thirty-year age difference, they fell in love, and married a short time later. After spending a few years together in Washington state, Lee and Snow made their home in Ho Chi Minh City.

After a weekend of learning a few words of Vietnamese to aid us when ordering food and acting as tourists with Lee and Snow, we made plans to join them in November at Snow's childhood home in the mountains where we could experience traditional Vietnamese life.

Armed with a handful of words, our confidence flourished. We explored many nearby restaurants and explored the city markets. Many of our evenings in Da Nang were spent at the beach. While the sand dunes and rolling waves always looked appealing, the beaches were deserted in the middle of the day. Had we opted for a midday swim, we most certainly would have been fried to a crisp by the scorching sun. But in the evening, as the sun dipped low on the horizon, the temperature cooled enough to enjoy sitting on the sand or splashing in the water. From our hotel, we simply had to cross the street to get to the beach. We'd walk along the water's edge until the boys decided it was time to dive in. Often, I would stay on dry land, enjoying the warm breeze while the boys splashed and jumped the waves.

One night, we walked further down the beach and came upon a stretch where many people were enjoying the waves in a roped-off swimming area. We decided that was the spot for the evening. Even though they didn't say as much, I could tell the boys were comfortable enough in their new setting to try some interaction with others, even if it was only swimming in a more crowded space. After Ray and the boys set out for the water, two women approached me and sat down on either side of me—literally, right next to me—while a man and child went to play in the waves. I was instantly on my guard. Robbed of my personal space, I was waiting to be robbed of my possessions. After all, I was a single white woman sitting all alone on the beach. In a foreign country. Realizing I had nothing worth stealing, however, I relaxed as they struck up a conversation.

As we spoke, the women scooched in tight as if we were close friends. "What your name?"

"Lisa," I replied.

Both women looked confused, so I drew the letters in the sand, L-I-S-A.

"Ah, Lisa." They both tried hard to produce an "L" sound.

"What's your name?" I asked.

"Bic," the woman on my left replied as she drew the letters B-I-C-H in the sand. I was glad she spoke her name aloud first, because I most certainly would have pronounced it "bitch."

I looked to the woman on my right, "And your name?"

"Hahng," she replied, also drawing the letters in the sand, H-A-N-G. Another name I would have mispronounced without the verbal cue.

Not being a touchy-feely person, it was uncomfortable for me to have the two women sit so close. We did our best to continue the conversation. Both women would gently touch my arm when they wanted my attention. Bich told me she'd learned English in school, but never used it unless she ran into tourists, usually at the beach.

"You like brown skin or white skin?" Bich asked, touching her skin and then mine.

"I like when my skin is tan . . . brown," I answered.

"My skin too brown. I like white skin most," Bich commented. "I want white skin like you."

She told me that in Vietnam, white skin was a sign of wealth and beauty, and people with darker skin were judged to be ugly. People who had white skin were inside all day and rich, while the people with the brown skin were those who worked in the fields all day and were poor.

We chatted through a series of broken English and pictures in the sand until our families returned from jumping in the waves. I said goodbye to these two women who wanted nothing more from me than conversation.

Covered in sticky salt water and sand, the boys needed to rinse off before our walk back to the hotel. An open-air facility between the beach and the street was located behind where we were sitting. Thinking the showers were open for public use, we walked up and rinsed off. The facility also had large pools filled with water where mothers would strip their youngsters naked and dump buckets of water over their heads. Girls and boys alike were stripped and rinsed, showing no modesty whatsoever. RJ and Tyler were a little shocked at the display and turned their heads, embarrassed for the kids.

Once rinsed, we walked through the park toward the street. Suddenly, a short man in a white undershirt and faded jeans rolled up to mid-shin stepped out from a center pavilion and yelled at us in Vietnamese.

"I don't understand. What's he saying?" The man shook a fistful of money at Ray and then pointed at him.

"I think he wants money," I said.

The man's voice became louder and louder, and he shook the money at us.

Ray shrugged and shook his head. "I'm sorry. No money."

We hadn't brought money to the beach. Eventually, the man gave up and shooed us off the property. We walked out the front gate, where we encountered a welcome sign, a sign we'd missed since we'd entered from the beach side. While we couldn't read the words, but we could decipher enough to realize we were required to pay a small amount to use the shower facilities.

We returned the next day, this time entering through the front gates. The same man spotted us and rushed up to us, again yelling words we did not understand. Ray pulled out enough money to cover the previous day as well as the current day and offered it to him apologetically. The man figured out we were trying to atone for any wrongdoing. His face brightened as he clapped Ray on the shoulder and stepped aside, allowing us entry to the beach through the facility.

"You know, I think I'm going to miss Da Nang," I said, as we made our way to the beach.

"It really doesn't feel like we've been here a month," Ray said. "Pretty cool place, huh?"

I nodded in agreement, then kicked off my flip-flops and dug my toes into the sand. "So different than I expected."

"Gives you a whole different perspective on Vietnam, doesn't it?" Ray asked.

"I'm definitely more at ease."

Once again, I was confronted with direct opposition to the views I'd held. Many evenings at the beach I'd been engaged in conversations with people who wanted to talk to me because I *was* American. They wanted to practice speaking English and learn more about me and tell me about the beauty of their country, excited I'd come so far to see it. Even when making mistakes, we were easily forgiven with a pat on the back.

Ray had warned us all to avoid eye contact when crossing the street, but I found when I had to opportunity to look someone in the eye, to spend even a brief moment in conversation, I didn't find any of the animosity I had expected. I wished my dad could have experienced the wonders unveiled, if only he could have had a different experience in this country.

Da Lat

The first leg of the four-hundred-mile journey to Da Lat started with a ten-hour train ride taking us as far as Nha Trang. From there, we had to take a bus into the mountains. Snow had informed us we needn't take the bus all the way into Da Lat proper, but said we should ask the driver to drop us off at the crossroad to her village, some fifteen miles before the main town.

As we boarded the bus, Ray approached the driver, but was stopped by the attendant—an aide who helped move people on and off the bus, schlep luggage, and generally act as gatekeeper for the driver.

Ray asked, "Can the driver drop us off at Trai Mat?"

"No," the attendant replied with a firm shake of the head and a stern expression.

Ray joined us in our seat at the back of the bus. "He won't stop for us."

"Did he understand what you wanted? Lee and Snow seemed sure the driver would stop for us. Maybe you should try again. Try fewer words," I said.

"I'll try again." Ray sighed as he made his way back to the front of the bus.

"Trai Mat?" Ray took me up on my suggestion to make sure his point was clear.

"No." The attendant slashed his arm, palm face down in front of his body, indicating the decision was final.

Ray returned, shaking his head.

"Okay, I'll let them know they should meet us in Da Lat." I sent a note to Snow before the bus departed the terminal letting her know the driver would not drop us off where she had indicated.

We settled into our reclining seats on our full-size tour bus—rivaling any Greyhound I'd ever been on—for an eighty-five-mile journey that would take over three hours, winding up five thousand feet of elevation on switchback roads. The cliffs grew ever steeper as we traversed back and forth, up and up. After a couple of hours, the vegetation gave way to cleared areas and buildings became more prevalent.

"We must be getting close." Ray pressed his head to the window.

And then, without warning, the bus stopped at a roundabout in the middle of an empty highway and the attendant pointed at us and then pointed out the door.

"Trai Mat?" Ray asked.

The attendant nodded his head and pointed at us again and then pointed out the door, his stern expression never varying.

"Um, I think he wants us to get off the bus. This must be the stop we asked for." Ray began gathering his belongings.

"But Lee and Snow will be expecting us in Da Lat. Should we stay on?" I asked, growing nervous we would not be where we said we would be. Not to mention, the bus had simply pulled over to the side of an otherwise desolate road. There was a roundabout, but little else.

"I don't think we have a choice," Ray said, as the attendant again pointed at us and pointed out the door, this time accompanied by stern words we didn't understand.

We gathered our belongings as quick as we could and made what felt like a walk of shame as if we were being kicked off the bus for bad behavior. The attendant opened the luggage compartment, and we pointed out our bags. He grabbed the packs and set them heavily on the sidewalk, then turned without gesture or comment and stepped back on the bus.

"Trai Mat?" Ray called after him.

We didn't appear to be in any village. We were surrounded only by terraced farmland to one side and a small road leading down the hill on the other. The attendant pointed toward the only other spur on the opposite side of the roundabout and closed the door. The bus pulled back onto the road and sped off toward town, leaving us in a cloud of dust and exhaust. And there we stood, four Americans at a roundabout along a quiet road, somewhere in the middle of Vietnam, the midday sun beating down, no one waiting to pick us up, and no Wi-Fi. We looked at one another and laughed. I had to admit laughing was a whole lot easier than panic.

"Well, what now?" Ray asked with a little chuckle.

"I guess we go that way." I pointed to the road across from where we stood. "We should try to find a place with Wi-Fi so I can let Lee and Snow know what happened."

"I'm sure they'll figure it out when we don't get off the bus in Da Lat," Ray said.

We strapped on our packs and walked down the road, feeling, and probably looking, completely out of place. The first building we came to appeared to be a service station straight out of the 1950s, with a small counter selling cold drinks and packaged snacks. No one spoke English, and all heads were turned in our direction as Ray's voice grew louder in trying to get the men at the counter to understand what we needed. I pulled out my phone and pointed to the Wi-Fi symbol, showing it all around. The men shook their heads and pointed further down the road.

"Well, that was some quick thinking. See, you are pretty good under pressure when you're not fretting," Ray said.

Another mile down the hill, the town took shape as more shops lined the street. Cars began to pass this way and that, and we encountered more people on the street who mostly stared, confirming we were indeed an anomaly in this small village of five thousand. We came upon an ice cream and coffee shop advertising free Wi-Fi. The boys ordered a scoop of ice cream while I got connected and shot off another message to Snow detailing what happened and our current location.

"I'm hoping that's enough for them to find us." I felt bad about sending Lee and Snow all over town in search of us.

"We'll be fine, Mom," Tyler said. I smiled at his reassurance, happy to see his confidence return.

Within fifteen minutes, Lee and Snow pulled up in a minivan laughing at the whole caper. They had been waiting in town when the bus pulled in. They watched as passenger after passenger unloaded, waiting for us to appear. When no Americans disembarked, they asked if anyone had seen four Americans. Apparently, whatever the passengers had said gave them a chuckle, and they quickly figured out that the bus had let us off at the village crossroad looking like deer in the headlights, wide-eyed and unsure of which way to turn. Lee and Snow joined us for a scoop of ice cream and then we were carted off to meet Snow's family.

We drove away from the village of Trai Mat to an even smaller area where houses were surrounded by tracts of farmland on rolling hills and pieced-together greenhouses constructed from various types and colors of material. As we turned onto a dirt road, Lee pointed out the land where Snow's father and youngest brother worked together on their acre of land growing coffee and anthurium flowers—upside-down, heart-shaped, red, waxy flowers.

"Where are the flowers?" RJ asked.

"We can't see them from here; they're in a greenhouse. I'll take you there after we get settled," Lee replied.

The van turned onto a dirt road and then into a long sloping driveway. We were greeted by Snow's father, two brothers, their wives, and a two-year-old niece, all lined up awaiting our arrival. Snow's family did not speak any English, so we were introduced to them with the help of translation by Lee and Snow.

As we entered the home, we were given instruction on shoe protocol. In traditional Vietnamese homes, there is a defined set of rules about what shoes can be worn inside versus outside. This home had plumbing, but the toilet and shower were in a small building off the back porch, outside the main home. Outside shoes cannot be worn inside, and inside shoes cannot be worn to go outside to the toilet. Upon entering the home, you must exchange your outside shoes for inside shoes or bare feet. When a trip to the toilet is in order, you must leave your inside shoes at the door and change to outside shoes to walk to the toilet. You then must leave your outside shoes at the bathroom door, and step into bathroom shoes. With your bathroom duties complete, you must reverse the entire process, even taking care to exit the bathroom in reverse, leaving the bathroom shoes pointed in the correct direction for the next occupant. I would challenge Cong's only difference between Americans and Vietnamese. Add shoe usage to kissing and peeing.

Once we were clear on the house rules, Lee took us on a tour of the home and explained it had started out as a small, one-bedroom home but had been expanded over time to five bedrooms. The warm tones of the wood floors and walls gave the home an inviting feeling. The tour continued outside as we walked down the hillside to see the coffee beans and greenhouse. Although I'd been a coffee drinker my entire adult life, I'd never seen a coffee plant. The beans grew in clusters along the stem of the plant in varying shades of green, yellow, red, and brown. Our last stop was the greenhouse, just below the family home. Lee led us into a large, fenced area surrounded by a heavy cloth on all sides, providing both air circulation and shade for the flowers. Bed after bed of anthurium flowers stood so uniformly sized and shiny they looked fake.

As we returned to the house, Lee asked RJ and Tyler, "Want to help catch dinner?"

"Catch dinner?" RJ asked, confused about the question. "Like, go fishing?"

Lee laughed. "We're having chicken, but first we need to go catch a couple in the henhouse."

With wide eyes, the boys went off with Lee to corner the chickens. Once captured, the boys opted out of helping to kill the chickens but stood on the back porch watching from a distance as Lee drained the blood into a bowl and then soaked each carcass in boiling water to help with feather removal. The blood was taken inside to the kitchen for use the next day and covered with a cloth to keep the flies out. I didn't ask how exactly it would be used; I wasn't sure I wanted to know. Ray jumped at the opportunity to de-feather the birds, saying, "When will I ever get to pluck feathers from my dinner again?"

In rural Vietnamese homes, I was surprised to find that even in 2015, many families still cooked outside over open charcoal fires in clay cooking stoves the size of large coffee cans. Tyler and I offered to help prepare one of the dishes—Vietnamese pancakes. To make the pancakes, we first heated a small amount of oil in a small pan, fried up mushrooms, squid, and shrimp, then added a rice flour and egg mixture. The batter was topped with chayote squash and covered until cooked.

While we cooked, Lee and Snow transformed the living room by moving furniture to the sides of the room and spreading mats on the floor. Fifteen people—our family of four, Snow's family of eight, and three neighbors, whom I suspected were invited to dine with the American family—sat in a circle around the mat with the dishes spread out in the middle. The savory egg omelets tasted delicious, maybe even more so since we had had a hand in preparing the meal.

As we wiggled around, trying to find a comfortable position for our legs, Lee pointed out that we were sitting right in front of the infamous desk that had blinded and maimed Snow.

I wondered how a desk could be responsible for her missing hand and blindness. I had assumed, incorrectly, that Snow's disabilities had been the result of birth defects.

"When this house was much smaller and Snow was young," Lee started, "she studied very hard. But her parents often had guests in the evening and they all sat at the kitchen table to talk. This left Snow without a place to study. Her father told her if she got straight A's for a year, he would buy her a desk. The following year, holding to his promise, her father went to the military warehouse to get her a desk."

"What's a military warehouse?" RJ asked.

"When the American military withdrew from Vietnam, they left a lot behind. All the office equipment was gathered and placed in a warehouse and sold to the Vietnamese people very cheap—desks, file cabinets, office chairs."

Lee continued, "Her dad brought home a desk and present- ed it to Snow. She was so excited to have a desk of her own. She set about cleaning it right away, as it had been sitting for years and was covered with dirt, grime, and spiders. She was almost finished when she spotted a small area under the top with a few lingering cobwebs. The space was too small for her hand, so she grabbed a wire hanger and poked it into the space to clear the webs. As she did this, there was an explosion."

"Oh my gosh! What was it?" I hadn't seen that coming.

"No one knows. No one else was in the room when it happened. The neighbor," Lee said, pointing to the man sitting next to her father, "who had the only vehicle in the village at that time, helped get Snow into the city as fast as he could, but she lost her hand and was blinded by the explosion," Lee finished.

I looked at Snow's father, surrounded by his family and friends, happy and content. He had brought a product from the war into his home that had permanently injured his only daughter. Yet, he allowed Snow to marry an American man, a veteran of the Vietnam War. He had invited and welcomed an American family into his home. Was he ever tormented by the memory of the explosion? Did he ever cast blame and carry resentment like an overladen backpack? If he had suffered as a result of his part in this story, he had left those feelings in the past. Blame and regret were not guests at this dinner party.

If only we shared a language so I could ask him. Looking into his eyes, I saw only a generous man, happy to share his home with his guests. The only answer that made sense to me was that he'd found forgiveness—maybe for the desk saboteur, maybe for all Americans, maybe just for himself. He hadn't let his demons close in upon him as my father had. I realized, sitting there watching this man interact with his family with clear eyes and open body language, that Snow's father had found peace.

Ho Chi Minh City (Saigon)

Our final stop in Vietnam was Ho Chi Minh City. As a place central to the Vietnam War, Ho Chi Minh City was home to several museums. Outside the War Remnants Museum, all manner of Vietnamese and American planes, tanks, and vehicles used in the war were on display. Inside, there were graphic depictions of the torture inflicted upon the POWs showcased in small cells built to resemble actual prison conditions—the complete opposite from what was depicted at the Hanoi Hilton. This was the war I had envisioned all along.

The first room we entered was painted blazing orange and contained an extensive exhibit putting the effects of Agent Orange on full display. The contrast between the bright walls and the life-size black-and-white photos of children with birth defects hanging at eye level drew our attention to the details of each image. I felt the emotion building in the back of my throat. When I wandered near a case that held an embalmed unborn fetus with two heads, I knew I had to move on before the tears fell. My heart ached for those children, those who were still experiencing the effects of Agent Orange to this day.

The next room in the museum was filled with photos taken by journalists and letters from soldiers exhibiting all aspects of American involvement in Vietnam. Unlike the sparsely populated Agent Orange room, this room was filled with people wandering from image to image. The room was quiet, each person deep in his or her own thoughts. I walked through the gallery of letters and photos, studying each, hoping to see my dad among the soldiers. Their letters reminded me of one I had come across after Dad's death, postmarked from Vietnam, 1970. He wrote:

I am now at a base about five miles from Tay Ninh. It wasn't too bad when I first got up here, but now with the TET offensive coming up, it's getting quite hairy. We've been pulling day recons and night ambushes. We go on a couple eagle flights a week. That's where you get on a chopper and go out, land, check out an area, get back on and repeat a few times. Last eagle flight my platoon landed, and we got hit pretty bad. Six guys got wounded and we were pinned down. A gunship came in to help us and it got shot down. They sent in two companies and pulled us out. The other companies lost another gunship, three men and a couple more got wounded before they finally broke through the VC lines. It really gets scary when the lead is coming in your direction. I got so scared, I actually almost shit. I'm just glad I wasn't one of the ones that got hit. I've kept my shit together so far.

"So far" were the key words in his statement.

I looked at my boys—teens on the verge of the same age Dad was when he was sent to war. I couldn't begin to imagine them hiding in the jungles and killing others, dropping chemicals on mothers and children because the government ordered them to do so. But I could see how innocence would be lost with the first bullet fired and how that kind of trauma could stay with you forever.

Our second war memorial stop was a visit to the Cu Chi Tunnels—a network of underground tunnels in the jungle used by the Viet Cong as hiding spots during combat. Part of the tour led us through a portion of the tunnels. Struggling to walk in a crouched position in the increasing heat, Ty and I opted out at the first exit after about seventy-five feet, but Ray and RJ continued through the entire four hundred feet, the tunnel decreasing in size and increasing in heat the whole way. With not even enough room to navigate through in a crouched position, they had to walk in a squat through to the end, the only light coming from the guide's flashlight.

Tyler and I walked along the jungle trails toward the tunnel's end point, listening as machine guns fired in the distance. Part of the attraction for tourists at the Cu Chi Tunnels was the opportunity to fire the same type of weapons used in the Vietnam War. I closed my eyes and tried to imagine Dad in this same area—camping in the sweltering jungle, surrounded by hidden tunnels, the sound of machine guns firing from a location he couldn't quite pinpoint.

Ty looked at me and asked, "Are you okay, Mom?"

"Yeah, I was just thinking about a story my dad told me about the tunnels," I answered.

"What was it?"

"Well, after Dad and I saw the movie *Platoon*, he told me about a scene that was almost exactly the same as something he'd experienced. One night, he was on watch while the rest of his platoon slept. Scanning the jungle, he heard a rustling in the distance. He went to investigate, his gun ready. He and a Vietnamese solider came upon each other, suddenly face to face. Both raised their rifles and aimed at each other."

I paused before continuing, watching Tyler to gauge his reaction to the story. He was looking at me intently.

"They stood completely still and stared into each other's eyes, each waiting for any reason to pull the trigger. When neither of them fired, Dad and the other man walked away in opposite directions. Two lives had been spared. Dad said that in that moment, he saw the humanity of the other man, and all the killing that he'd been a part of crumbled in on him."

"What does that have to do with the tunnels?"

"Dad suspected the soldier had come out of one of the tunnels," I said. "If he'd been killed that night, neither of us would be here."

"Wow. That's intense to think about," Ty said.

I wondered if Dad told me about this, knowing it was the moment that broke him. How do you go from killing people in the remote jungles of Vietnam one day to fathering a baby girl the next? Before he was my dad, he was a nineteen-year-old boy ordered to march into another country and gun people down, see children killed and women raped, look death in the face, and watch his friends die all around him. How could a boy not even out of his teens go through these experiences and come out "normal" on the other side? The answer, at least for my dad, was he couldn't.

When Dad died, I rushed back to Montana to help my aunts and uncles clear through the detritus of my father's apartment and multiple storage units. Walking into his apartment, I saw he was a stranger to me in the last years of his life. Every inch of his apartment was cluttered with odds and ends he found valuable but which most people would call junk. Every flat surface, from windowsills to tables to countertops, was full of trinkets, overflowing ashtrays, and drug paraphernalia, confirming he had graduated far beyond marijuana. Weapons—knives and guns in all states of disrepair—were scattered about, a weapon within arm's reach from anywhere in the apartment. It was clear he had spent a lot of time in a state of anxiety, drugs his only elixir. I could imagine he felt alone in his struggle, that no one would understand where he'd been or the depths of emotion and internal struggle he was engaged in every waking second of the day.

Watching as Ray and RJ emerged from the tunnels, disheveled and dripping with sweat, I knew the boys had their dad firmly by their side. I was the one flaking out on our family, struggling to remain emotionally available. My kids would ultimately pay the price if I checked out. I didn't want them to experience the same loss I had. There was no way for me to repair the relationship with my dad. Reparation had to come in the form of breaking the cycle. I was no longer a daughter, but I was still a mother.

I looked at Ray and felt like I was truly seeing him. Not just as my husband, the goofball who made me laugh and loved me without restraint, but as the father of my children, the man I chose to walk the path of parenthood with. I knew without a doubt that RJ and Tyler would never be left at the window waiting for Ray to show up. And I knew he would never let his own fears get in the way of being a father.

In the final scene of *Platoon*, as Charlie Sheen's character is flown out of the area via helicopter, he sobs as he stares down at craters full of corpses. In his closing words, he says, "I think now, looking back, we did not fight the enemy; we fought ourselves. And the enemy was in us. The war is over for me now, but it will always be there, the rest of my days . . . ." The war certainly remained with my dad for the rest of his days as I'm sure it did for many soldiers, the emotional toll rippling into future generations.

I was more determined than ever to move forward.

Days of Travel: 89
Miles Logged: 16,686

LOSING CONTROL

Phnom Penh, Cambodia

I remember reading that the difference between fear and excitement was about two inches—the physical distance between the place where fear tends to tie your stomach in knots and the place where butterflies flutter about in excitement. Both emotions have the same physiological effect on the body. During the six-hour bus ride from Vietnam to Cambodia, my fear held the butterflies struggling to take flight captive. Even after three months of travel, entering a new country continued to produce anxiety. I closed my eyes and focused on relaxing, hoping that by calming my body, my mind would follow. I imagined my personal guardian deity, which had morphed into a combination of the monk who blessed us and the statue representation of my guardian in the Buddha Tooth Relic Museum in Singapore. He held a bat in one hand and a lotus in the other, as if to say: *If I can't find peace, I will beat the darkness off with a stick.*

My fear was a biological response to help me deal with danger, but what danger was I facing? In Vietnam I'd been afraid people would think negatively of me as an American. I was happy I'd been mistaken on that point. And yet, I kept coming back to the fear of how I would be perceived. By allowing these concerns to overpower my thought process, I was giving my power away. The power to think about myself in a positive light, the way I guessed most people thought about themselves most of the time. At some point during The Glitch, or maybe even before that, I had allowed my self-identity to be hijacked.

Reclined in the plush seat of the touring bus, I made the decision to act out of a place of excitement rather than fear. In Cambodia, I would look at my life and be excited by the possibilities, act with determination, and feel confident I was making informed choices. It was time to reclaim my confidence, return to my sense of self.

We arrived in Phnom Penh, the capital of Cambodia, and found a tuk-tuk to take us to our hotel. The boys were excited to ride in the three-wheeled, motorized vehicle with a motorcycle in the front and a covered carriage for passengers in the back. Nothing went wrong—our luggage was not lost, we were safe and made it to the hotel without issue. I still felt out of place, but rather than letting dread rule the day, I embraced my unease and paid more attention to my surroundings.

Compared to Vietnam, Phnom Penh was less developed—the streets worn down and strewn with garbage. Many roads were unpaved, even in this capital city, the buildings older and more dilapidated. Perhaps after almost two months, I'd adapted to the pace and rhythm of my surroundings in Vietnam, only to jump into a new adventure, and I missed the familiarity I'd left behind.

We settled into our hotel and Ray and I began the now familiar process of researching what kinds of adventures we could have.

"How long do you want to stay in Phnom Penh?" I asked Ray as we searched the Internet.

"I don't know. Why?"

"I'm just trying to look forward to the adventures rather than letting the new-country jitters take over," I said. "Having a bit of a plan helps."

"I think I can guess where RJ gets that trait from." Ray flashed a cursory smirk and went right back to his research. "You'll be fine."

"Look at this," he said, turning his laptop toward me.

"Oh, we have to go there." This was one culinary adventure we were all sure to remember.

Without telling the kids too much, Ray and I took the boys to lunch at a place specializing in rural Cambodian cuisine. The restaurant served as a training ground for former street youth or those who came from other marginalized and at-risk groups. The goals for student staff were to learn new skills that would allow them to get into the workforce and improve their lives.

I made sure RJ and Tyler both saw tarantula on the menu. After an initial shock, the boys were game to try the deep-fried tarantula appetizer. Tyler even decided to embrace this culinary experience and ordered the red tree ant soup.

"What do tarantulas taste like?" RJ asked the waitress as we placed our order.

"Chicken," the waitress said, without missing a beat.

None of us expected her next question, "Do you want to see the live tarantulas?"

"Like, before they're cooked?" Ray asked.

"Yes. We have some to hold."

"Um . . . okay," Ray answered with mixed anticipation and hesitation before I could even wrap my mind around being at the same table with live tarantulas. Deep fried tarantulas were one thing. Live, gigantic, furry spiders mere inches from my person were another.

The waitress returned to our table a few minutes later with a small white saucer and an upside-down cup in hand. She set the plate on the table and then lifted the cup to reveal two tarantulas the size of eggs cuddled together with their spindly, black legs intertwined. The spiders were completely still on the saucer and we couldn't tell if they were alive or dead. Perhaps they were in shock from seeing their cousins dropped into pools of bubbling oil.

"Are they alive?" I asked, wondering aloud what we all feared.

"Yes." She picked one up and held it out for us to take. My adrenaline spiked as Ray tentatively extended his hand while asking, "Is it safe? Do they bite?"

"Only if threatened. But their venom is weak." She placed one spider and then the second in Ray's open hands, none of us questioning her definition of "weak."

I've never been particularly fond of spiders. The spiders I'm used to, however, are smaller than a dime and don't have fangs, at least not that I could see without a microscope. These tarantulas were far too close for my comfort. With an urge to scream, I backed my chair away from the table with a jerk. I hurried to the other side of the table to put some extra distance between me and the hairy beasts. Now far enough away from the small monsters, I pulled out my camera to document the dread creeping over Ray's face as one spider crawled up his arm, heading right for the gap between his sleeve and flesh, perhaps to nestle in the warmth of his armpit.

"Okay, you can take them back," Ray said, his eyes imploring the waitress to remove the spiders.

She gently lifted the spiders from his arms and cradled them in her hands. "Does anyone else want to hold them?" She showed no discomfort whatsoever as she offered the spiders to each of us in turn. I guessed she had faced far scarier things in her life than a spider crawling up her arm.

Our heads all shook in unison. There was no way the rest of us would touch those spiders.

"Where do you get them?" Ray asked.

"Suppliers capture the tarantulas in the jungle," she replied. "People in the jungle eat them all the time."

A few minutes later, the waitress returned with a plate of three deep-fried tarantulas and a side of black pepper lime sauce. Who in the world determined that black pepper and lime were the perfect accompaniment to tarantula?

We each broke off a deep brown leg, dipped it in the sweet, tangy sauce, and tentatively bit into the appendage. They had the crunch and taste of overcooked French fries. Then we turned to the spider's abdomen.

When cutting the rubbery body part proved futile, Ray and Ty each took hold of a spider belly and popped the whole thing into their mouths in one go. They chewed and chewed and finally grabbed their drinks and washed down the masticated bodies.

"Well?" I asked.

"Definitely didn't taste like chicken," Ray said, with flecks of the black body and hair lodged between his teeth.

"More like digested insects," Tyler added.

"Not super enjoyable, but not altogether disgusting either," Ray said.

I noticed how we were all growing on this adventure. Not even a month before, Tyler was hesitant to sit among the crowds in Hanoi to eat. Now he was ordering red tree ant soup and eating tarantula. Even RJ, although equally hesitant to hold a tarantula as he was a scorpion, wasted no time in breaking off a leg and giving it a taste test.

When the rest of our meal arrived, we all took turns trying the red tree ant soup. Compared to the earthy, bug-infested, grittiness of the tarantula, the soup was a delightful combination of cucumber and lemon flavors. The ants didn't have much taste, but they added a pleasant, rice-like texture to the soup. Tyler hit a small roadblock when he spied a queen ant, five times bigger than the rest of the ants, in the bowl of his spoon. But, eventually, he closed his eyes and gulped it down.

As the tarantulas and red ants wriggled through the web of our digestive systems, we made our way through the streets of Phnom Penh and came upon a performance hall decorated with posters that caught my attention.

"The Cambodian Living Arts Theater." I pointed to a poster at the entrance. "Look, there's a performance tonight. The Plae Pakaa dance show. Should we go?"

Ray and the boys were quiet; they didn't seem enthused by the thought of a dance performance.

"C'mon, we might learn something. I'd really like to go," I pleaded.

That evening, we filed in with the crowd and sat on short wooden benches facing a small stage. As each dance began, a narrative was projected on an overhead screen, presenting a brief history of the Cambodian struggle and what the dance represented.

In the first performance, several women came onto the stage dressed in traditional wrap skirts, jeweled tops, and elaborate head dress inspired by the Apsara images representing the female spirit of the clouds and water on the Angkorian temples. As the musicians played traditional Cambodian music—a mix of xylophone and drums accompanied by a somewhat discordant stringed instrument—the women danced with precise movements and deliberate steps, upper torso moving only slightly, their wrists, hands, and fingers bent backward at seemingly impossible angles.

Overhead, the description read: *In 1975, the Communist Khmer Rouge took control of Cambodia. The goal of the party was to implement a radical Maoist and Marxist-Leninist transfor-mation program, turning Cambodia into a rural, classless society in which there were no rich people, no poor people, and no exploi-tation. To accomplish this, they abolished money, free markets, normal schooling, private property, foreign clothing styles, reli-gious practices, and traditional culture . . .*

This regime had stripped the people of their identity, almost rendering it extinct. The casualties: beauty, art, innocence, and self-direction. But this troupe of artists was taking back their heritage, regaining their autonomy one act at a time. I wanted to believe I, too, could take back my sense of self, but damn, it was hard to fight for that power when the opposition was a ghost in my own mind. I took Ray's hand and gave it a squeeze, taking comfort in his warmth radiating into my palm. I was still among the living. I would fight as long as I remained that way.

In one of the final acts, two dancers performed the Dance of the Golden Mermaid, symbolizing an epic legend about the struggle between good and evil. The female was clad in an out-fit with silver lines representing scales and fins. The male was dressed all in white and wore a monkey mask and chased the Mermaid around the stage.

In a three-year time period, thousands of intellectuals, city resi-dents, and minorities were executed. The Khmer Rouge forced two million people from the cities into the countryside to undertake ag-ricultural work. Thousands died and many others were held in pris-ons, where they were interrogated and tortured. One prison held fourteen thousand prisoners . . . only twelve people survived.

Walking home from the theater that night, the city took on a different feel. I was no longer intimidated by the darkness or worried about who I might pass in the street. I had a new per-spective on Cambodia. This was a nation of people rebuilding their lives, people who were the living embodiment of for-giveness. When you hear the word "genocide," there are so many details you don't consider. The national story took on new meaning when I focused on the individual lives affected. The people of Cambodia had taken responsibility for the future of their lives and for generations to come. In fewer than forty years, the Cambodian people had moved from having their entire lives stripped away to reclaiming their relationships, homes, and culture. While I would guess there were many people who gave up when they lost everything, so many more chose to fight to regain their identity.

Holding Ray's hand as we made our way back to the hotel, I realized I was the only one responsible for what happened next in my life. Who I had been in the past didn't have to be the same person I would be in the future. I was the only one repeating the same story for myself, day after day, not letting fear morph into excitement. I continued to give the voices in my head far too much control over how I behaved and what I believed to be true about myself. It was time to change the story and decide what role I would play in my own life.

Battambang

Breaking up the ten-hour journey from Phnom Penh to Siem Reap, we stopped midway in a small, out-of-the-way, French colonial town called Battambang. It's funny, the little places that draw you in with a short description on a travel blog. Had we missed the description, we might have passed right by. Based on our limited Internet research, we expected to be met by a pack of kids looking to pick our pockets when we got off the bus. We were not warned about the blaring music videos sung by Cambodia's version of John Denver playing at max volume for the entire five-hour bus ride. By the time we hit Battambang, we didn't care what was left in our pockets to pilfer through, we just wanted off the bus.

When the bus pulled up to the drop-off point, there were no kids in sight, only a group of tuk-tuk drivers ready to deliver passengers to their chosen hotels. Drivers had their rates posted on their vehicles. From my window seat, I made eye contact with a driver and waved him over.

Stepping off the bus, I handed my backpack to the driver as Ray looked on.

"No, wait." Ray shook his head and put up a hand to stop me. "Lisa, what are you doing?"

"It's okay." I took Ray's hand. "He'll take us to our hotel."

"But, we haven't negotiated the price. The site said they could charge us way too much," Ray protested.

"It's okay," I repeated. "His rate was posted on his tuk-tuk. It's two dollars. We're all good."

Ray had failed to notice the drivers, their posted rates, and my silent conversation of eye contact and nods with the driver as we arrived. I smiled to myself, noting my calm and collected demeanor.

Once at our hotel, we unloaded our backpacks. The driver showed us a brochure with local activities. Several caught our attention and we asked him about pricing. He said he would take us on the city tour, to the bamboo train, and to the bat caves—acting as our tour guide all day for twenty dollars. He seemed nice enough and wasn't pushy, so we agreed.

Yaya arrived in front of our hotel the next morning promptly at eight thirty. The sun was already blazing and there was not a cloud in the sky to ease the rays. On the way to the bamboo train, Yaya gave us a running commentary about his city and his history.

"Your English is really good. How did you learn to speak English so well?" I asked.

Yaya told us he was trying hard to complete college, but it was very expensive. He gave tours for a year to make money, then returned to school for a year, then repeated the process. His determination to work hard and get an education was inspiring. The voice inside my head chastised me for lingering so long in grief and anxiety when, in comparison to Yaya, I was living a life of luxury. I had let my sadness overshadow my whole life.

As we pulled up to the bamboo train, Yaya explained that the route was developed by resourceful survivors of the Khmer Rouge in the early 1980s. They utilized sections of the remaining intact rail after the Khmer Rouge pulled up much of the original track to prevent the Cambodian people from escaping.

"Where is the train?" RJ asked, looking around for familiar-looking train cars.

"This is the bamboo train." Yaya pointed to the tracks.

The "train" was a simple bamboo platform atop two heavy sets of wheels and axles not unlike a homemade go-kart. An old motorcycle engine mounted on the rear axle provided power. A three-inch-wide band, not unlike a super-sized drive belt, placed over the rear axle and attached to the rotor propelled the platform. The tour guide used a stick to stretch the band, creating more tension and greater speed. Slowing down was a reverse of that process. Nothing but careful placement of the bamboo frame and gravity held the conveyance together as it sped down the warped track.

We climbed aboard the bamboo train, sitting on mats and pillows, the four of us taking up most of the space on the frame. When we were situated, the driver used his stick to stretch the band and we raced down the track at thirty miles per hour. The ride started out nothing short of exhilarating with a little terror thrown in for fun.

"Is that another train coming toward us?" Tyler asked, pointing.

The trains sped toward one another on the single track, then slowed until the cars met. Everyone on the returning train disembarked and the drivers worked together to lift the contraption—frame, motor, and each axle—off the tracks. The driver then reassembled the vehicle after our train moved forward. With construction complete, both trains were once again on their way.

Once we realized we weren't in imminent danger of crashing into another car, we settled in to enjoy the Cambodian landscape, marveling at how peaceful it felt to be rolling through the rice paddies without another soul in sight, only occasionally getting whipped in the face by overhanging branches and errant spider webs. After a short stop in a village at the end of the line, we returned to the depot where Yaya waited to continue the tour.

"Do you want to stop at a crocodile farm?" Yaya asked on our way back to the hotel.

We looked at one another with raised eyebrows. "Sure!" Ray said.

Our family was transforming from hesitant risk-takers to enthusiastic adventurers. Unfortunately, in our ignorance, we envisioned a crocodile conservation or sanctuary protecting the animals. We entered a neighborhood of small houses and shacks and walked up to a ten-foot-high wooden gate where Yaya knocked. We heard the gate unlatch from the opposite side and squeak as it opened just wide enough to see who had knocked. Perhaps this was a safe haven, but not for crocodiles.

Inside, an old woman dressed in a shabby housecoat led us to the side of the main house where seven baby crocodiles baked in the sun at the bottom of a black rubber pan. She spoke quickly while Yaya translated. She picked one up indicating how to hold the critter to avoid getting chomped. As the demonstration progressed, the boys noticed the baby crocodile wasn't moving much and Tyler asked, "Is it dead?"

The woman shook it back and forth, and when sensing no movement agreed it was indeed, dead. She placed it on a shelf and motioned us farther into the property where cement pit enclosures were loaded with hundreds of dusty green, ten-foot-long predators wading in deep green, fetid water. So many crocodiles inhabited this small space that they engaged in a constant fight for wiggle room and often rested on top of one another.

Approaching the overlook, Yaya asked, "Do you want to feed chicken to crocs?" He pointed to a cage of squawking chickens. I really hoped he was kidding.

Thankfully, Ray responded, "No."

The woman in the housecoat led us up a set of stairs to a walkway, no wider than two feet, spanning the crocodile pits. She ambled right across and waved for us to follow—no guardrails, no safety precautions, nothing to stop us from taking a twenty-foot dive into the pens.

"Ray, this is definitely *not* safe. Let's go!" I wondered if the crocs could smell the fear radiating from me as I turned slowly and walked back down the stairs. "Boys, come back down. Carefully." I heard an echo of my mother's voice asking what the hell I was doing letting them walk over a pit of crocodiles.

Driving back to the hotel, I was annoyed at myself as much as Yaya. I felt irresponsible for introducing the kids to such a cruel practice and letting Yaya lead us into potential danger. But, I decided to find out more. "Is crocodile farming legal?" I yelled over the hum of the tuk-tuk.

Yaya glanced over his shoulder and smiled. "Yes, in Cambodia. But the farms are struggling. Bringing tourists to visit the farms helps the owners continue operations."

I glanced at Ray, who just shrugged. "I don't understand how that's okay."

Yaya maneuvered the tuk-tuk through the streets while keeping up an explanation of the farming practice. "There are around four hundred thousand crocodiles in the area on seven hundred farms. And there is an agreement between governments to make sure they are not threatened."

RJ had been watching the volley between Yaya and me, and asked, "What do they do with the crocodiles?" Crocodile skin purses and necklaces made of crocodile teeth in town flashed through my mind.

"The farms sell hatchlings to farmers in Vietnam or sell the crocodile leather to China," Yaya answered.

He pulled up to the hotel so we could take a break during the heat of the day.

"I'll be back to pick you up at four." Yaya waved goodbye.

Back in the room, my first order of business was to look up crocodile farming practices in Cambodia. I learned about CITES (Convention on International Trade in Endangered Species of Wild Fauna and Flora), an international agreement which aims to ensure that international trade in animals and plants does not threaten their survival. Yaya was not contributing to illegal farming practices but doing a small part to help his neighbors' industry and livelihood survive. I felt ashamed for having been so quick to judge the situation. The fear of my family falling into a pit of crocodiles had dictated my reaction and blocked all reasoning. I was glad I'd taken the time to investigate further.

Yaya returned to gather us for the tour to the killing caves as the sun started its descent. The tuk-tuk chugged along the flat expanse of the Cambodian rice fields, larger vehicles speeding past us. I worried if we'd have enough time to explore but decided to trust Yaya. There was no rush, and this was a familiar journey for him. Yaya explained that he used to be a guide at the killing caves and was learning more about

Cambodian history in his college classes. A lone limestone mountain, out of place in the otherwise level landscape, edged ever closer as we spoke. Since dusk was not far off, we opted to drive to the top of the mountain, rather than climb nearly thirteen hundred steps. Passing people drenched in sweat on the way up, I was confident we'd made the right choice. Three spires of a Buddhist temple topped the peak. A row of golden Buddha statues draped in saffron robes perched on a stone wall looking out over the plain far below. We walked through the trees to the top of the peak while macaque monkeys jumped from tree to tree overhead, on the lookout for any food or shiny objects they could snag from unsuspecting tourists.

Standing near three gaping cracks at the summit, Yaya explained, "The Khmer Rouge would take people to these openings and throw them in. Sometimes they would cut off their heads or stab the people before pushing them over the edge. One cave was for women, one for men, and the third for children. Some people survived the sixty-foot fall but died later from injuries or from having no food and water." Yaya paused before continuing, his features tightening. "The Khmer Rouge were most cruel to babies. They would smash the babies' heads against this large rock and then toss them down into the children's cave."

A shiver ran through my body as I looked at the boulder, the middle stained dark with what I imagined had to be blood. I glanced at RJ and Tyler to gauge how they were handling this information and saw that they both looked shocked to hear about the brutality that occurred here. When Ray and I decided on a tour of the killing caves, I had hoped for a history lesson. I wanted the boys to know about the Cambodian genocide, to feel and understand the suffering that took place here. Now, I considered this might be too much for them, although reading about the Cambodian genocide in school would not have carried the same weight as standing in the very place the atrocity occurred. Even though I had learned about the Khmer Rouge in school, I had never imagined anything this brutal. I was gaining a deeper understanding and I decided not to be too hard on myself over the choice to explore this area.

After a moment of silence, Yaya led us to the base of the killing caves. We followed several other groups down a long limestone stairway carved into the hill. Everyone was silent out of respect for those killed here and the brutality they suffered. Green vegetation and low-hanging vines covered the rock walls, adding to the closed-in stillness around us. A huge golden Buddha reclining on his side dominated the cave interior. A smaller room opened to the right, where a glass enclosure the size of a large elevator was filled with human skulls. Looking up, we could see the hole in the cave's ceiling hundreds of feet above our heads where we had just stood. I traced the victims' paths as they took their last breaths before hitting the stone floor, right where we were standing. The atrocities that had taken place in this beautiful spot suddenly became all too real and emotionally overwhelming. RJ and Tyler, caught up in the heaviness of the moment, moved closer on either side of me and I took hold of their hands and squeezed, reassuring them I was present.

Yaya directed us out of the cave and led us to a rocky outcropping to watch the sun set, and let the crisp greens and browns of the landscape and the brilliant oranges, pinks, and purples of the sunset calm our hearts and minds. We spread out on the rocks, giving one another space to digest the experience in our own way. I looked at Yaya in silhouette on a rock with praying hands in front of his chest and head bowed. I wondered how difficult it was for him to repeat this story day after day. Perhaps this prayer after the tour was his way of flushing the bad memories and returning to strength. In his own way, Yaya was giving me a new appreciation for not only the struggle of the Cambodian people, but the way in which they now made their way through the world—connecting to and understanding the atrocities of the past, but not letting the actions of the Khmer Rouge continue to instill fear.

As the sun's last rays disappeared, Yaya drove us to the base of the mountain and parked the tuk-tuk along the road where another immense cave, its entrance a hundred-foot fissure in the limestone mountain, swarmed with millions of bats, very much alive.

This solitary mountain in an otherwise flat landscape was home to extraordinary death and teeming life. Cambodia continued to strike me as a place of duality—life and death, war and peace, chaos and harmony.

We sat on a rock wall and waited with a group of a hundred other tourists for the sky to darken enough for the bats to head out on their nightly foray. Each time the boys spied a bat leaving the cave, they pointed it out, excited this might be the start of the exodus.

"Just wait," Yaya said, "you'll know when it really starts."

And sure enough, the single bat turned into two and then twenty, then two hundred, then ten thousand. The bats were departing the cool of their cave *en masse*. We stared at the sky with a renewed sense of wonderment as millions of bats poured out of the rugged mouth in a twisting and churning column, seemingly apart but always together, setting off in a line across the sky to eat their fill of insects.

The bats have no control over their environment; they exist and hunt according to the setting of the sun, their own internal instincts. They rely on themselves and one another, each creature playing a part in the strength of the colony, helping to keep it functioning.

"Keep your mouths closed, unless you want to sample the bat nectar," Yaya reminded us. That was not a sprinkle of rain speckling our faces.

Riding back to our hotel, we looked out over the land and watched the line of bats stretching for miles, as far as we could see, in the fading light. They flew on, not turning back until they'd had their fill or until the dawn came again, not dwelling on the past or fearing the future, but living only in the moment.

Siem Reap

In contrast to Battambang, where there were few tourists, Siem Reap was a tourist mecca. People from around the world flocked to see the Angkor Archaeological Park, just four miles north of the city on a site measuring over four hundred acres. I was ecstatic to be visiting Siem Reap, a place I had long dreamed of visiting.

I had read about the Angkor temples when I was young, poring over the pages of a *National Geographic* magazine, studying each curve in the carved sandstone buildings, tracing each tree root growing on top of and through the walls, imagining myself standing in awe of the architecture and the gigantic trees towering above me in the jungle. I read the accompanying descriptions over and over, memorizing as many details as I could about this mysterious place.

The Angkor site was spread out over such a large area, it would have been impossible to see everything in a single day, so we purchased a three-day pass. Our tuk-tuk driver would often drop us off at a temple and indicate where he would pick us up, typically on the opposite side, allowing us to walk through the buildings at our leisure, climb to the top of some and look out at the surrounding jungle. The architecture was like nothing I'd ever seen. Nearly every surface was ornately decorated with bas-relief friezes, apsaras (female spirits of the clouds and waters in Hindu and Buddhist culture), and devatas (stone carvings of males and females representing forest spirits, village gods, keepers of river crossings, caves, and mountains). Large holes dotted the walls where rubies, emeralds, and sapphires once glimmered in candlelit passageways.

I had a hard time trying to wrap my mind around the fact that these structures were almost a thousand years old, constructed some eight hundred years before Lewis and Clark set out on their two-year trek from St. Louis to the west coast of North America. The buildings were more than six hundred years older than my entire country.

Angkor Wat, the central temple in the complex and only one of hundreds in the area, was built in the early twelfth century and has remained a significant religious center and a symbol of Cambodia, even appearing on its currency and national flag. The temple was surrounded by a moat, a consistent thirty-nine-feet wide, representing the oceans surrounding the world. Moving inward from the moat, a fifteen-foot-high stone wall measuring just over two miles in length surrounded the temple. Three rectangular galleries, one built on top of the next, were designed as a pyramid representing the structure of the universe. The highest level represented Mount Meru, the home of the Hindu gods. At the center of the galleries stood five towers, representing the five peaks of the mountain, the center tower reaching nearly seventy feet up from the top gallery. In 1586, Antonio da Madalena, a Portuguese friar, said, "[Angkor Wat] is of such extraordinary construction that it is not possible to describe it with a pen, particularly since it is like no other building in the world. It has towers and decoration and all the refinements which the human genius can conceive of."

By the early afternoon, we were all tiring of walking in the heat. "Let's sit for a minute." I pointed to a group of large stones in the shade.

Making our way to the stones, we inadvertently stepped behind a photographer taking a selfie.

"Sorry," Ray said, but the young woman just smiled and waved him over, handing him her camera and communicating through a series of gestures that she wanted him to get a better picture of her with the backdrop of the Angkor towers.

The boys and I continued to the shade and watched Ray communicate with this young woman through the universal language of photos. After he took her picture, she again waved him close and they took selfies together. Then, the tour group she was with, all enjoying their antics, began taking pictures of the two of them. They both reveled in the attention and posed for several minutes for the group, the entire crowd cheering them on. They twirled and posed while cameras flashed—stars in their momentary spotlight.

"Why does he always do that?" Tyler asked.

"Maybe we should be asking why we're too embarrassed to join him," I answered.

In this moment of silly behavior right in the center of the main temple, I remembered this was the goofball I fell in love with, the man who made me take myself a whole lot less seriously, who made me laugh. I didn't want to shame him for being himself or place undue restraint on him. Mock him occasionally, maybe, but not condemn his behavior. His lightness and goofiness—his model of taking life as it came—was exactly what made me desire to always be with him. I needed to stop shaming myself, too. This was what being at peace with oneself looked like, modeled right in front of me all along.

Of the many temples we visited in the Angkor complex, my favorite by far was Bayon. The most distinctive features of this temple were the two hundred and sixteen serene stone faces jutting out from the otherwise flat towers, smiling down upon me. While there is debate about whether the faces represent Buddha or King Jayavarman VII, all the faces have the same calming effect on the onlookers. I felt a new sense of peacefulness as I wandered through the temple.

Feeling negative in this tranquil environment was impossible. The faces served as a powerful reminder that I was worthy, I would be okay, and I was enough. Or maybe it was my guardian deity beating back the fear.

I looked up at the faces, weathered gray stone against a blue sky, and knew I had to stop beating myself up for not being what someone else thought I should be or for what my mom had told me I wasn't. Now that both of my parents were gone, the only way left to experience the connection between parent and child would be with my own children. To look upon them lovingly and unconditionally with no expectation or need to control them. To give them the voice of reassurance that could echo in their minds. To be present.

I gazed into the stone carving and relaxed my stomach, letting the butterflies free to flutter about, releasing my fear and embracing the excitement. I was ready for a new story. I was meant to be here. Now. Standing among the faces of Bayon Temple and letting the power of the two hundred and sixteen faces smiling down upon me sink into every pore.

Days of Travel: 99
Miles Logged: 18,435

FINDING BALANCE

Yangon, Myanmar

Four months into our adventure, we were becoming more accustomed to the routine of entering a new country. From getting through customs and obtaining visas to finding a taxi and getting to our hotel, we sailed through our entry into this sprawling city of nearly six million. Though the country of Myanmar had been under a military dictatorship from 1962 to 2011, and closed to tourism, the country was beginning to step into its own as a major destination.

As had become our routine, we wanted to get out and interact with this new place right away. Even though we had read that Myanmar was the safest country in Southeast Asia, I noted a sense of discomfort in my kids as we walked through the streets in search of dinner. Poverty was more visible in Yangon than any previous city we'd visited, and litter was abundant. Undeterred by our human presence, rats dug through piles of garbage and debris piled behind our hotel and in alleyways along our route. Many people we encountered wore a pale yellow sunscreen made from tree bark on their faces and arms, giving them a masked appearance. Chewing on betal nuts and spitting the blood-red byproduct was so prevalent that streets, sidewalks, and users' teeth were stained a reddish-black. The result was intimidating, as if we'd walked into a horror movie, an entire city of ghouls staring at us with menacing faces and blood-stained teeth against a backdrop of garbage and rats.

"Mom, let's turn back and eat at the hotel." I could hear the unease in Tyler's voice.

"We're okay, Ty. I think we're just not used to it yet."

Instead of turning back, we reassured the kids and talked about the differences we were all noticing, deciding it was only our own preconceived ideas that had us feeling off. We relaxed into the walk and began to noticed more people saying hello and smiling.

The restaurant we'd been searching for, famed for Shan noodles—a specialty of Myanmar—turned out to be a small room just off the street with space for only two tables. When we arrived, a man waved us in and set out stools for us. He pointed to a bar where we had a choice of chicken or pork cooked in tomatoes. Once we'd decided, he served the meals over a bed of fresh, handmade noodles.

"This is really great," Ty remarked. "We should try something new every day."

I had to laugh at his quick transformation. "Isn't that what we've been doing?"

"Yes, but I mean besides temples," he replied, clearly worn out by three days of trudging through Angkor Wat.

Ray and I exchanged a glance. "Ty, we're actually headed to see a temple after dinner. Well, pagoda, really, or stupa," Ray said.

"What's a stupa?" RJ asked.

"Look it up on your phone," I replied. RJ surfed from site to site, giving us little snippets of information.

Although built with different materials, all stupas are of similar construction. Each sits upon a square base whose four sides refer to the four qualities of mind basic to the attainment of enlightenment—love, compassion, joy, and equanimity. The base is traditionally filled with jewels, precious texts, and relics. Five steps rise from the foundation and represent the progress of the mind toward enlightenment. A rounded, bell-shaped form on top of the steps contains a room for meditation or, if smaller, is filled with further representations of Buddha's mind. An ornamented spire, traditionally carved by a monk and wrapped in precious materials, is fixed to the base and protrudes through the top of the structure to reach its highest point.

"Sounds sort of interesting, I guess." Tyler shrugged and returned to slurping noodles. "But why are we going so late?"

"We're trying to time it so we're there at sunset. The pagoda is covered in gold and appears to glow in the evening light," Ray said.

"Real gold?" RJ asked.

Ray shrugged. "I think so."

After our early dinner, a taxi dropped us off at the front entrance to Shwedagon Pagoda, one of the most sacred sites in Myanmar for Buddhists and possibly the oldest stupa in the world. The entrance to the site was a twenty-foot-wide, covered stairway lined by thousands of cubicles overflowing with visitors' footwear. We removed our socks and shoes and began the three-hundred-foot climb to the top of Singuttara Hill. Once we emerged from the stairway, our view was dominated by the pagoda—2,600 years old, 367 feet tall (nearly 40 stories), the gold glowing in the rays of the setting sun.

"Wow," I said, the only word I could come up with. Ray and the boys nodded in agreement, also at a loss for words.

While the main stupa was the focal point, sixty-four smaller pagodas encircled the shrine and four larger temples marked the four cardinal points. A placard informed us that the lower portion of the stupa was plated with more than twenty-one thousand gold bars. The next sign described the tip—too high for the naked human eye to see in detail—set with 5,448 diamonds and 2,317 rubies, sapphires, and other gems, 1,065 golden bells, and, at the very top, a single 76-carat diamond.

We all stood for a moment, trying to catch a glimpse of the sparkling jewels.

"Look at that tiny figure at the base." I pointed to a monk clad in saffron robes.

We watched as he circled the base of the stupa, much like watching an ant circle a large hill. I wasn't sure any of us could comprehend the size of the monument had it not been for the ant-like monk.

The next morning, while the boys slept, Ray and I slipped out to find a tourist office to investigate our travel options through Myanmar. Looking through brochures we found an adventure we thought would be a once-in-a-lifetime opportunity and decided to book the trip. Although it would take us several days and a few stops to reach our destination, we agreed that viewing the two thousand temples of Bagan from the vantage point of a hot air balloon would be an adventure we'd never forget.

"Let's make it a surprise for the kids," I said.

"Okay, are you sure you can keep it a secret that long?" Ray asked, knowing secrecy was not my strongest quality.

"I won't say a word."

Mt. Kyaiktiyo (Golden Rock)

The first stop outside of Yangon started with a four-hour mini-bus ride to Mt. Kyaiktiyo at breakneck speeds, reminiscent of our drive to Ha Long Bay in Vietnam. I felt some apprehension speeding past burned-out skeletons of passenger vans crushed on the side of the road. I considered my own existence, the thin veil that exists between life and death.

Eventually, I just closed my eyes and listened to our guide, Mya, tell us about the history and legend of Golden Rock. The boulder appeared to defy gravity, precariously balanced on a granite slab. At twenty-five-feet tall, the rock was almost as tall as a three-story house and had a circumference of fifty feet. It was completely covered in gold leaf and topped with a stupa. Mya told us about the legend that the rock was perched on a single strand of the Buddha's hair. Mt. Kayaiktiyo had been a Buddhist place of worship for twenty-six hundred years. While the rock overhung the ledge by half its length, it somehow continued to balance at the extreme edge, surviving weather, erosion, and earthquakes.

We arrived at a staging area at the base of the mountain, a pole building large enough to house dozens of dump-truck-size vehicles, and a platform lined with several more trucks. A line of people waited to board. Mya led us up the platform and haggled with the truck loaders to get our group seated in the same row of the truck bed. The trucks had been fitted with benches consisting of a four-inch-wide wood slat to sit on and a metal bar that served as both a backrest for the row in front, as well as a handhold for clutching.

As the truck rolled out of the pole building, I elbowed Ray. "Look at that sign!"

A large billboard swinging overhead indicated our ticket price of 2,500 Kyat (approximately 2 US dollars) included life insurance. I wondered how often claims were made.

Ray shrugged. "Too late to back out now," he said, with a wink. "We'll be fine. We've got The Force on our side."

The ride up the mountain was like taking a ten-mile, vomit-inducing roller coaster ride with numerous hills, switchbacks, and drops to make your stomach flop. I was not looking forward to the ride back down. I took small comfort in not spotting any burned-out dump-truck skeletons on the side of the road.

Once at the top, we unloaded and filed to the entrance to pay our entrance fee. Everyone in our group removed socks and shoes and placed them in an appointed locker.

"Why can't we wear socks and shoes?" RJ asked, as we began our walk up the hill.

Mya explained, "It's about respect and a little about superstition. Some believe that if you don't take off your shoes, it's a sign of disrespect and you will experience negative karma. But, again, there is nothing in Buddha writing about removing shoes inside temples."

Mya had informed us of the many rules—mostly for women—when entering a temple in Myanmar, and we thought we had come to this one prepared. I wore mid-calf capri pants and a wide-strapped tank top. I knew I would have to cover my shoulders, so I also brought along a sarong to cover up during the visit. Mya said the length of my pants was sufficient, but when we passed through the gates, I was denied entry. I was made to use the sarong as a skirt over my pants and put on a light hoodie to cover my entire torso. The female guard was nice enough to use my sarong and dress me appropriately while the rest of my party waited. The males were able to get away with shorts and T-shirts, but I was doubly covered and sweating through my layers. I was thankful the sun, too, was shrouded.

"I'm sorry they made you cover up," Mya, said as we made the hour-long walk up the hill. "When we get to the top of the mountain, you three can visit the rock," she explained, pointing at Ray and boys. "But we are not allowed to cross the bridge," she said, nodding toward me.

We continue walking up a brick paved road lined with small shops on our way to see one of the most revered Buddhist pilgrimage sites in Myanmar.

"Why are women not allowed?" I asked, disappointed but interested, nonetheless, to see a rock so large it required a bridge to access.

"I don't understand why they let only males cross the bridge. Nothing in any Buddhist teachings differentiates what a man can do versus a woman. Buddhism promotes equality and balance. This rule of only men being allowed is stupid."

I had to agree with her. The rule didn't make sense to me, either, but I was only beginning to understand how much more personal freedom I had as an American compared to women around the world.

When we reached the rock, I held onto all backpacks, hats, and electronics from my family of males.

"Sorry, Mom," Ty said.

"It's okay, Ty." I smiled to reassure him.

I watched as Ray and the boys crossed a short wooden bridge and waited their turn to get close enough to add gold leaf to the rock. I snapped some pictures but stopped after a few clicks and stowed my camera, content to watch their hands delicately add gold leaf to boulder as if pressing too hard might cause it to tip it over the edge. I pressed my body against a cool stone wall with the hope of dissipating the heat building up under my layers. I studied the rock and thought about how easily life's delicate balance can be thrown off when challenges arise. I reminded myself that I hadn't toppled, despite how close I had felt to the edge. Four months into the trip, I felt confident in Myanmar—a country that had only been open to tourism for a handful of years.

We spent some time at the top of the mountain, content to be spectators and watch men and women alike pay homage to this holy site. As we began our walk back down the hill to the trucks, we passed a group of young females who giggled and pointed in our direction.

"They are wondering what kind of in-laws the two of you would make." Mya nodded toward Ray and me. "They find your sons handsome and would like to know if they are married."

"Sorry, they are only teens," I replied. "Far too young to be married." Though I did wonder if that were true in Myanmar.

Tyler's cheeks flushed as Mya relayed the information to the group of admirers who responded with a collective sigh.

When we reached the bottom of the hill, Mya said, "Congratulations, you have made your first pilgrimage. Look on the path you took today as a reflection of the life of a pilgrim. However comfortable the journey was for you is representative of the emotional baggage you are carrying."

I thought about not just this day-trip to Golden Rock, but the entire four months of travel thus far as my pilgrimage. Though I wouldn't have said so when we embarked on this trip, I was a traveler on a spiritual journey—a pilgrim. I had longed for a way to escape my life, but I found that what I really wanted was to step back into normalcy as a wife and mother, not be a parental spectator. I was no longer anxious about every detail but beginning to relax and pass that confidence on to my children. I still had lessons to learn, lessons to teach. I decided that I was well on my way to gaining confidence on this pilgrimage. I hoped that also meant my emotional baggage was waning.

Nyaung Shwe/Inle Lake

The only way to get to our next destination, the town of Nyaung Shwe on Inle Lake, was by overnight bus. We arrived at the "bus station" in the evening and found it consisted of a sectioned-off dirt road where packs of vendors were all selling seats on the same bus, packs of dogs were running rampant, packs of kids were trying to shoot birds out of trees with plastic pellet guns, and everyone was staring at us. As we passed the vendor shacks, I felt as if we'd been dropped into a Wild West movie. We were the strangers walking into town. All conversation ceased, dogs ran for cover, and babies started to cry as the dust swirled around our boots. But we made it onto the bus without incident.

I watched my boys recline their seats and settle in to get some rest. But I couldn't sleep. Maybe it was the anticipation of a new location, or how the bus careened around each switchback, making me feel like I was on the verge of rolling down the mountain side, or the Coke I felt compelled to drink at a 10:00 p.m. pit stop, or the Burmese folk music videos blasting on the TV until well after midnight, or the frigid A/C that never ceased, or the chemically infused aerosol that blasted from the front of the bus at measured intervals, scorching my nostrils. Maybe I just wasn't tired. Despite all the chaos on the bus, my mind was not spinning with worry. Instead, I was focused on my pilgrimage and this journey bringing my family together.

Around two o'clock in the morning, the road straightened, the music was turned off, and passengers quieted and started drifting off. Right as I started falling asleep, Ray shook me awake and said it was time to get off the bus. We had arrived. Not Nyaung Shwe, but another outpost ten miles outside of town. My watch read 4:15 a.m. We'd expected to arrive around 6:00 a.m., so Ray and I questioned the bus attendant several times, making sure this was, in fact, where we were supposed to disembark.

Reassured this was our stop, we sleepily gathered our things, unloaded our bags, and watched as the bus disappeared into the night. Whether it was the right place or not, we had arrived. Not used to traveling with so little information, we had come to rely on The Force to find our way.

Several men stood around fires burning in fifty-gallon drums. When one man noticed us shivering in the cool night air, he waved us over to the fire. "Come. Warm yourself."

We joined the group standing around the fire and discussed our next move.

"What time is it?" RJ asked, his eyes puffy with sleep.

"Not even five," Ray answered. "Do we have reservations somewhere?" Ray looked to me for an answer, the default hotel booker since Singapore.

"Yes, but not until tonight." I had expected to get to Nyaung Shwe early in the morning, but not this early. "I thought we'd be able to check in around eleven."

Overhearing our conversation, the man who had invited us to warm by the fire intervened, "I can take you to hotel, no problem. Bus always early."

The picture became clear. This was why the men were standing around fires at four in the morning. They were taxi drivers waiting for the bus to arrive so they could shuttle and drop off confused tourists.

"What is your hotel?" he asked.

I scrolled through my phone and gave him the name.

He nodded. "Good. They will be okay with you coming early."

Ray and I looked at each other and silently agreed this was probably our best option. I was happy to be in agreement on what we needed to do next. It felt nice to have a partner in the decision-making.

When we pulled up, we found a darkened building behind a locked security gate. As if it were the middle of the day and not predawn, the driver hopped out and rang a bell and yelled a few times. Two sleepy young women peeked out the door and then shuffled to the gate to unlock it. They asked if we had reservations, and I said we did . . . but not until that night. They invited us in, anyway.

While one woman took our information, the second carried a mat big enough for two into the lobby. All the rooms were full for the night, so we'd have to sleep where we could. She indicated that two people could sleep on the mat in the lobby and she motioned to a small room behind the desk just big enough for a couple of bodies. Ray cocooned himself under a blanket on the lobby mat and was asleep before his head hit the pillow. When I lay down next to him, however, I realized I didn't have my sweatshirt. I had been using it as a pillow and had left it behind in my groggy rush to get off the bus. The lobby floor was near the open doors. Cool morning air seeped in though the cracks and I was chilled. Since Ray was already asleep and wrapped up so tight that no heat could escape, I moved into the closet and snuggled in with the boys. There was enough room for all three of us if we slept on our sides. I never imagined being packed in a closet could be so inviting and warm. I had to admit that being so close to my sons filled my soul. We had long ago moved beyond the days of cuddling, but I had to believe that the closeness brought all of us some comfort.

Sitting in the airport at the Travis Air Force Base, back before the trip had begun, I had worried about situations just like this night—being dropped off on the side of the road in the middle of the night, not knowing where to go or how to get to our destination, not having a place to sleep, and not being able to communicate. This was the first time in four-and-a-half months of travel such a scenario played out. The result did not resemble the horrors I had imagined at all. Instead, people came to our rescue when we were in need. I could not have anticipated my greatest fears would lead to such a magical moment. There was a system here, even if it was not obvious to me.

Long before The Glitch, Ray and I had often talked about retirement and where we might spend our golden years. Southeast Asia had been on his radar. During our months of travel from city to city, country to country, he'd ask what I thought about one town or the next, but at first, I hadn't been able to imagine that far ahead in my life. I was stuck in the whirlpool of grieving, unable to stop long enough to think of the future. Although I'd enjoyed getting to know some thirty new cities on this trip, I couldn't see myself making a life in any of them. Until we visited Nyaung Shwe, that is.

A small town on the north banks of Inle Lake, Nyaung Shwe was where most tourists started their lake adventures. One main paved road ran through town lined with shops, restaurants, travel agencies, and a market. Most other roads leading to homes and guesthouses were dirt, only a few with makeshift sidewalks. A bridge at the edge of town spanned a canal where boats could be hired for lake tours.

Walking from our guesthouse to find a meal or visit the market, we passed homes and shops where a young man or woman sat on the front steps strumming a guitar and singing. Not for money or attention, but simply as an expression of joy. The smiles on the faces of the many shopkeepers and business owners were infectious. People in the town seemed genuinely happy just to be. From the moment we were taken in at the guesthouse in the middle of the night and sent to sleep in the closet for a few hours, everything about this place felt right.

Once caught up on sleep, we opted for an all-day tour of the Lake. Inle Lake—the second largest in Myanmar—measures forty-five square miles, its deepest point only reaching twelve feet. However, some seventy thousand people live in four cities and numerous small villages along the shore, and in stilted settlements on the lake itself. Our first sight after departing the docks in Nyaung Shwe were the fishermen. Each man stood on the bow of his narrow boat, one leg rotating the oar and propelling the boat along, while the other kept him balanced, leaving his hands free to cast his net into the lake. Even the fishermen in Myanmar practiced a delicate balance.

Next, the tour made stops at several lake villages where we saw many industries at work—silversmithing, boat-making, blacksmithing, umbrella-making, lotus-silk-thread weaving, wood craft, and cigar-rolling. A floating garden the size of a football field, formed from lake-bottom weeds and anchored by bamboo poles, supplied fruits and vegetables to the surrounding villages. The garden was resistant to flooding due to its ability to rise and fall with changes in the water level.

After lunch at a stilted restaurant near the garden, the tour took us up a tributary to the village of Indein and the thousand stupas. This site was accessible by boat only in the winter months when the water level was high enough to allow passage.

I smiled at our remarkable luck and the timing of our visit to Myanmar in December. The boat passed through a series of man-made half-dams, the river level gaining almost a foot at each dam, much like a fish ladder.

Once in Indein, we explored through the village to the outskirts, where we wandered around old, crumbling shrines with trees and roots growing in and around the structures, contributing to their decay. Looking through the opening of one stupa, we found a half-buried Buddha surrounded by bricks that had fallen from the surrounding walls and caved-in ceiling.

"This can't be the thousand stupas. There's not even a hundred," I said.

"Look over there." Ray pointed to a long, covered walkway winding half a mile up the hill and disappearing into the trees. "Let's see if that leads anywhere."

Climbing the hill, I noted a few shrines that were less decayed. When we reached the top of the hill, stupas dominated the landscape as far as we could see, set against a backdrop of lake and mountains under a clear, blue sky.

"This is the place," I said with confidence.

The older constructions near the entrance of the complex were made of mud and stone, some intricately carved. The newer stupas, painted gold and constructed with precious metals, were found near the back of the site. Small bells atop each stupa chimed in the light breeze.

"I feel like I've walked into a fairy tale." I had never felt so captivated by my surroundings.

The red brick of the temples absorbed the light and gave off warmth, the white-and-gold stupas reflected the sun, giving them an angelic, glowing quality. The tinkle of the bells led me to imagine the sound of a magic wand sweeping through the air.

Ray and the boys moved through the grounds while I stopped to read about the history of the site. It was believed to date from the third century, B.C. Monks were sent across Asia to spread Buddhism. A pair of monks found their way to this area and built the temples. Said to represent Buddha's holy mind, the temples showed the path to enlightenment. Building a stupa was a powerful way to purify negative karma and accumulate extensive merit. The repetition of the purifying negative karma message was not lost on me. All through Southeast Asia, the message of purification kept coming into my consciousness, the repetition taking the place of the negative echoes in my mind.

I caught up to Ray, who was reading about the significance of the number one thousand. "Read this one," he said.

It is believed that if one makes a thousand stupas, they will become a great 'Wheel-turning Holder of the Wisdom Teachings' and have clairvoyance knowing all the Buddhadharma. After death, without being born in the lower realms, you will be born as a King. You will become like a sun, rising in the world, with perfect senses and a beautiful body. You will be able to remember past lives and see future lives.

"Oh, I like that one. I want to be reborn with perfect senses and a beautiful body," I said.

"Oh, you got that going on already." Ray gave me a sly, mischievous look.

I gave him a little shove and laughed. But I had heard him more than I let on. Even in my darkest days, Ray had seen past my exterior into the depths of my heart. We walked together and caught up with the boys near the back edge of the complex, where hundreds of gold spires surrounded us.

"Mom, listen to this," Ty said, reading a plaque. "The 'Stainless Beam' mantra states that all negative karma and obscurations are purified even by dreaming of a stupa, seeing one, hearing the sound of its bells, and, even for birds and flies, by being touched by its shadow."

"What's obscurations?" RJ asked.

"Look it up in your thesaurus," Ray answered.

RJ typed the word into his thesaurus app: "Shadow, blackness, darkness, obscurity."

"That even sounds like a fairy tale," I said. "It's like magic. Negative karma and darkness are purified simply by hearing the bells or touching the shadows. I love it." I felt touched by the energy of this place.

I studied each curve and edge as I passed, lingering an extra moment in the shadows. I memorized the gentle ringing of the bells so I could replay this scene in my mind any time I felt darkness creeping in. This was my moment to remember . . . a moment to bring inner peace—the feel of the warm sun on my skin, the cool of the shadows, the soft chiming of the bells, the beauty of the white, gold, and red temples against a blue sky.

As we began our walk back to the boat, I said, "Ray, I don't ever want to leave here."

Myanmar was a place where I felt lightness. I was letting go of the negativity which had blanketed me for so long.

"If I ever disappear without a trace, you will probably find me in Myanmar," I said. "But I guess that sort of defeats the purpose of disappearing if I tell you where I'm going."

"I'll just have to make sure you never have a reason to disappear." Ray put his arm around me and pulled me in close.

Bagan

We'd been told we were entering the "high" season for touring Bagan, but the town was quiet, with few tourists about. Bagan had been the capital city of the Pagan Empire from the ninth to thirteenth century. In that time, over ten thousand Buddhist temples, pagodas, and monasteries were constructed, more than two thousand of which still existed in varying states of repair, connected by a web of trails and dirt roads.

With temples spread over forty square miles, the best option for visiting the temples was via e-bike—much like a moped or motorized scooter in the States, though with less power and speed. Rentals were available around town, and at our hotel.

"You ride e-bike before?" the young man in charge of rentals asked me as we lined up in front of the bikes. Ray and I had decided on just two bikes, each being responsible for carrying one of the boys.

"Oh, yes," I said, stepping astride the bike.

I'd driven scooters before and had my own motorcycle when I was a teen. A scooter seemed similar enough to an e-bike to make this assertion. I was more concerned about Ray's ability, as I'd once seen him almost crash a four-wheeler when he couldn't figure out the throttle.

"Good." He reached out to tap my right hand. "The accelerator. And the brakes," he said, flapping the paddles on both sides of the handlebar.

I looked at Ray to see if he was absorbing the infomation. I wasn't sure he'd ever been on a scooter. But the young man was intent on giving me instruction, perhaps assuming that, as a man, Ray had already mastered riding an e-bike.

"Great." I nodded. I waited for him to walk back inside before turning to Ray. "You sure about this?" I asked.

"Got it," he said, with a knowing smile. "And they're electric bikes, so I'm guessing their top speed is like fifteen miles an hour. Nice and slow."

My eyes widened as I pictured Ray and Tyler crashing into a wall at fifteen miles an hour. I let the thought go and said,

"Okay." I waddled my bike into the road, RJ's weight behind me throwing me off balance.

We set out slowly down the dirt road from our hotel toward the main street leading to the temples, Ray and Tyler on the lead bike, RJ and I following. Without a look back, Ray made a quick right-hand turn. I made a stop and started to turn right but felt like I would tip over, and instead, straightened out and sped straight across both lanes. Thankfully, there were no cars in either direction, allowing a clear path for my mistake. I quickly got our bike pointed the correct way, looked left and right, and started off again, racing to catch up.

Just as we had Ray and Tyler in sight, RJ noticed a dog running across the road a few feet ahead of them. "Uh-oh," he said.

I slowed the bike, expecting Ray to slow and make room for the dog to cross, but he kept on at full speed. Within seconds, he and the dog had collided, and we heard a loud yelp. Ray pulled over and I pulled in behind him.

"What are you doing? Why didn't you slow down?" I asked, as upset about being left behind as I was about the dog.

"I didn't think the dog was dumb enough to run out into traffic. I thought he'd stop."

"Where did he go?" asked RJ.

We looked around to see if the dog was okay, but he had already run off. Within the first five minutes of our e-bike rental, I had almost run off the road and Ray had hit a dog. Thankfully, we both got the hang of driving with a few miles of practice.

On the e-bikes, we were able to reach distant temples. Sometimes this meant driving along dirt roads with patches of deep sand, impossible on a bicycle, but only somewhat treacherous on an e-bike. We discovered Ray and I had two distinct riding styles. When Ray hit an unstable patch of sand, he would speed up, drift a bit, wobble, and regain control before dumping himself and Tyler off the bike. As I hit the same unstable patches, I would let out a little yelp, hit the brakes, and then struggle to get started again in the sand. Although there were no crashes, and we made it to our destinations unscathed, this was reminiscent of how we handled problems.

While tourists in Bagan visit the larger and more popular temples, navigating our own way on e-bikes allowed us to visit smaller, distant temples, often being the only visitors.

"Do you think it's okay to explore inside?" I asked Ray, as we arrived at a temple with no one else in sight.

"I don't see why not," he said, already beginning to remove his shoes and socks.

We set our footwear outside the main entrance and entered the dark hallway, the interior lit only by small holes in the walls, letting in natural light.

"Mom, look, here's a set of stairs," Tyler called to me, his voice echoing off the bare interior. Ray and I joined the boys at the base of the stairs and started up.

The stairway was no wider than a single person, and the ceiling was low, making it necessary for all of us to stoop as we climbed.

Once we reached the top of the stairs, we exited onto an open landing circling the entire temple.

"Look, there's another level." RJ pointed to an open doorway and another set of stairs. "Can we go up?"

"Go ahead, we're right behind you," I said.

When we reached the second landing, we looked out over the land, now able to see the tops of hundreds of temples poking up through the trees.

"Wow. There are so many. Can we do this again, tomorrow?" Tyler asked.

I nodded. I could tell the boys were having a good time and I, too, was enjoying our independence in exploring. "Which one do you want to see next?"

Ray pulled out his map and we gathered around to decide and set our course.

When we returned to the hotel, I sent Tyler into the lobby to return the e-bike keys.

"Mom, the front desk asked me to give you this message," he said upon his return.

"Did you read it?" I asked, after looking at the message on the piece of paper and fearing our surprise might not be a surprise anymore.

"No, but the person said something about the van picking us up at five thirty tomorrow morning. We're not doing another sunrise thing, are we?" he asked with a sour face. Tyler had not enjoyed rising at 4:00 a.m. to watch the sun rise over Angkor Wat in Cambodia.

"Sort of," I said.

Tyler's mood instantly deflated. I looked at Ray with raised eyebrows. I couldn't contain the secret any longer.

"Go ahead, you can tell them," he said.

"Well, when we were in Yangon, we booked a trip to see the sunrise over the temples of Bagan. But this time we are going to see the sunrise from hot air balloons," I said.

"Really?" RJ asked.

Tyler's face brightened. "We get to go in a hot air balloon?!"

The whole mood of the room changed to one of excitement.

We were picked up before sunrise the next morning and taken to a field where we were fed coffee, tea, and pastries while we waited for the light to arrive. Thirteen balloons were being launched, and the passengers buzzed with excitement as the large balloons were unfurled. The sky began to lighten and crews filled the balloons with warm air by blasting jets of fire into the openings. The colorful orbs gradually rose from their horizontal positions, until they were floating above their much smaller passenger baskets.

"Okay, we're ready to board," our pilot announced.

She described the loading procedure and went over safety precautions. Then, she instructed us to climb into the basket and take a seat in preparation for takeoff. Once the basket lifted a few feet off the ground, we stood and looked out at twelve other balloons all rising together, taking off into the calm, predawn sky.

"Mom, what floor would this be in a building?" RJ asked, trying to gauge just how high we were.

"Oh, probably like two hundred. But I don't think there are any buildings that tall."

Thinking about that number put our elevation in perspective. We were higher than the tallest building in the world, in a basket attached to a giant bag of hot air with little sound other than the burner's jet heating the air. We drifted over the temples for more than an hour, rising as high as two thousand feet.

"It's so still up here, I expected it to be windy," I commented to the pilot.

"Many people say that," she replied. "But we are moving at the same speed as the wind, so it feels still even though you would feel a breeze if you were standing on the ground."

My life had been moving in such a way that I felt constantly knocked around by the harsh winds of life. The trick, I could see, was to rise above it, to float along at the speed of the wind and not let it whip me out of the sky. To find balance. Perhaps, although I hated to admit it, to be more like Ray, going with the flow rather than against it.

As we drifted, a sense of peace came over me. I was letting go of the past that had been pulling on me. I would never forget my departed family, but I was learning to stop feeling guilty and wishing circumstances were different. The roles these lost family members had played in my life had ended and I'd learned from all of them. I couldn't change the past. The best I could do would be to learn from it.

I looked at Ray and my boys standing still, each gazing out over the landscape, floating above the world. We were the square, the four sides of our family stupa, all in balance. This was my new base from which the rest of our lives would take shape. The four sides—love, compassion, joy, and, finally, equanimity.

"I'm not sure we're ever going to top this adventure." Ray looked at the other balloons silhouetted against the rising sun.

"Where are we going next?" RJ asked.

"India," I answered.

Tyler thought for a moment, then asked, "Will we get to see the Taj Mahal? That might be pretty cool."

Ray and I looked at each other and smiled. We were creating two adventurers. Though had I known the chaos India had in store for us, I might have opted to stay in Myanmar.

Days of Travel: 116
Miles Logged: 20,707

THOUGHTS OF HOME

New Delhi, India

Our first sign of trouble started at 3:00 a.m. at the Bangkok airport when our flight to Delhi was delayed for several hours. We got in line behind a young Indian couple and waited for the ticket counter to open and an agent to relay our new departure time. Ray struck up a conversation with the pair right away, somehow always "on," even in the early morning hours.

"Are you waiting for information on the flight to Delhi?" he asked.

"We've been waiting for an hour," the young man answered.

"We got an e-mail notifying us of the delay, but it doesn't look like they got the message." I tilted my head toward an angry mob forming just down the way, everyone in the crowd pushing to get closer to the counter. I wondered if they were upset about more than the delay.

"Indians always think they need to be first or they will be left out," the young woman said. "That is why we moved to Thailand—to get away from the daily struggle just to function."

"We were told India would be a tough country," Ray said.

She looked at us with narrowed eyes, as if to assess our level of resilience. "You might find it challenging, but it's worth the trouble. There are beautiful places in India."

Often, when people we met in our travels asked us about upcoming destinations, I'd mention my excitement for India. I was almost always met with concerned looks from those who'd experienced the country. One fellow traveler said if India were a video game, it would be level ten. Neither Ray nor I gave much weight to these comments. After all, how hard could it be?

As soon as the ticket counter in front of us opened, the mob we'd been watching rushed in front of our small group—as if the plane would only take those who got tickets in the next five minutes. They vied for the same information, despite several security and airline personnel asking everyone to move back. I was elbowed out of the way by a short, older woman in a sari, her face tight, showing no sign of apology. We joined forces with the young Indian couple, rearranging ourselves into a straight line, shoulder to shoulder, firmly planted to prevent any additional luggage carts from maneuvering in front of us. Regardless of our position in line, the message was the same—the flight was delayed for several hours.

Similar scenes continued throughout the morning. Each time the gate agent started to make an announcement, passengers scurried to line up at the door before they heard that the flight had been delayed ... again. When the announcement was made to begin the boarding process, the mob raced again to be first on the plane. Our family of four stood back and watched the spectacle unfold. We waited until everyone else boarded before moving to get on the plane. Though the passengers on the flight were quiet, there was a palpable tension that I sensed could be unleashed any second.

When we landed and Ty stood up, a girl seated two rows behind him climbed up and over the seat to get in front of him and closer to the door, which wasn't even open yet. Exiting the plane, the mob battled to be first to the baggage carousel. We stood back, waiting to see our backpacks before entering the melee. When our bags slid onto the rotating carousel, I noted all of the carabiners that had been attached to the exterior were missing. Since we were traveling with only one bag each, carabiners had become an important addition. We used these clips to latch extra bags or wet shoes to the outside of our packs when they wouldn't fit or couldn't go inside. Though this was not a substantial loss, my frustration was growing.

When we finally stepped outside the airport, we were struck by a cacophony of horns, taxis, motorcycles, and people swirling in every direction, like a hurricane that doesn't know which way to blow. If it weren't for their height and familiar clothes they'd been wearing for four months, I would have easily lost sight of my three men once we stepped into the chaos.

I'd known there would be poverty and begging along India's streets. I knew it would be unlike any other place we'd experienced, but I never imagined I'd feel so overwhelmed by the disorder and confusion surrounding us. The bustling Indian world I'd concocted in my head had not included blaring horns, pushing and shoving, and angry shouts coming from every direction.

The boys and I stood in a tight knot on the sidewalk while Ray flagged down a taxi. When the car pulled up, I leaned into the passenger window and handed the driver a piece of paper with the name and address of our hotel. "Do you know this hotel?" I asked.

Along with pre-booking a hotel in a new city, I'd also learned to write down all the hotel information for taxi drivers in case we encountered language barriers.

His head wobbled from side to side. Was that a *yes* or a *no*? Somewhere in between? His gesture did not instill confidence.

I looked at Ray. "What do you think?"

Ray asked again, "Do you know where this hotel is?"

"Yes, yes." The taxi driver waved his hand for us to get in. We had to either trust this man to take us to our hotel or jump back into the competition for another taxi.

After leaving the airport, the taxi made several stops along the way. Each time the driver took my piece of paper with the hotel address to another driver and asked for directions. He turned onto a busy market street and pulled to the side of the road. He then jumped out of the taxi and moved to the trunk of the car to remove our packs.

"I guess this is it. Let's go," Ray said.

I got out of the car and looked around for our hotel sign.

"You're sure this is it?" I asked the driver.

"Yes. There." He pointed down an alley, his head again wobbling back and forth.

"Ray, this doesn't feel right," I said, as the driver unloaded our backpacks from the trunk onto the street.

"Mom, everyone is staring at us," Tyler said. More and more people began to stop and a small crowd was gathering in a semicircle around us.

I looked for a friendly face I thought might be approachable to ask for directions, but there wasn't a face in the crowd that wore a smile. I felt like an intruder. The driver pointed down the dark alley again and then returned to his car and drove away.

"RJ, Ty, keep a hold of your backpacks," I said.

"See if you can pull up directions on your phone," Ray suggested, helping RJ with a twisted strap on his pack.

My phone hadn't worked in Myanmar, and so far, it wasn't finding a network in India, either.

"It's not working. Let's try the alley," I said.

We started down the alley, but at once felt closed in by the unbroken wall of buildings on both sides, the power lines and cables intertwined into a mass of coils overhead, shutting out the light. My instincts told me to turn back to the main street and leave this darkness.

Ray went ahead a bit, then returned. "I don't see it, let's go back to the main street."

Back on the street, we all studied the signs to see if maybe we had just missed the hotel sign. A man in a dingy red jacket approached us and asked if we needed directions. Ray asked if he knew where the Smyle Hotel was located.

"Yes, I know where it is, let me show you." He turned on his heel and led us through the market, in the opposite direction of the dark alley.

Ray and I looked at each other, both knowing that following this man through the market was as wrong as wandering down the alley. Ray shrugged, and we silently agreed to follow, not having any better plan at that moment.

"Ray, this isn't right," I complained as we walked, unconcerned whether the man could hear my protests.

He was far enough ahead of us by this point that I doubted he could make out my words over the noise of the busy market and the constant wail of horns from cars and tuk-tuks. I knew we were not in the right place, but I didn't feel scared like I might have earlier in the trip. Running on a few hours of sleep, I didn't have the patience to go on a useless trek. My tolerance was wearing thin.

"Probably not, but what else do you want to do? We don't know where it is," Ray said.

We trailed the man in the red jacket through the market.

"I feel like cattle being taken to slaughter." The new calm that I welcomed turned to anger. I became increasingly certain with each step that we were being led astray.

Ray chuckled, "There won't be any cattle slaughtered here. Cows are sacred in India. Isn't that evident by the cows roaming through the market and cow pies everywhere you look?"

I rolled my eyes as we stepped through a swinging door held open for us by our transient guide. Inside this small office, grimy plastic chairs lined the walls and worn maps hung limply from dingy walls. The man in the red jacket turned without a word and slipped right back out the door.

"Where is he going?" RJ asked.

"Apparently, we've reached the slaughterhouse," I said.

I looked around at the posters, each promoting a tourist destination and price. RJ gave me a quizzical look.

"I think he is a finder, RJ. He wasn't leading us to the hotel. He was bringing us to a tourist office. Maybe he gets paid for bringing tourists here."

"Well, we might be able to get a map." Ray said. "We can at least find the street we're looking for."

Another man who had been sitting quietly listening to our conversation said, "You need a map? This is not the right office. I know a better place, let me show you."

With no sign of immediate attention, every agent already engaged with other customers, Ray and I again shrugged and followed him out the door. The man led us into another tourist office a couple of doors down, and, just like the last man, once we were delivered, hewalked right back out the door.

"Come in. Sit down," said an agent behind a desk, neatly attired in a short-sleeved button-up shirt and tie.

We remained standing. "We just need to know where to find our hotel," Ray said, uncharacteristic frustration spilling over in his tone.

"How long are you in town? Do you have any plans?" the agent asked, trying a different approach.

"Can you point us to our hotel or—" Ray was interrupted by my phone, which had begun to chime repeatedly, indicating new messages.

It was working! Though it had taken its sweet time finding a network.

"What was that?" Ray asked.

I stepped away from the desk and punched the address of the hotel into Google maps. A blue dotted line popped up and plotted the course.

"Let's go," I said to my crew, ignoring the agent trying to engage Ray. "The map is working."

"Come back for best deal on tourist packages," the agent yelled after us.

We traced our steps around corners, back through the market to where we were originally dropped off. Two blocks farther on, we made a turn down another dark alleyway flanked by two open urinals and a line of men eager to empty their bladders. I hadn't thought it possible, but this alley was darker and dirtier than the first one we'd stepped into. Garbage cans spilled their contents, motorcycles held together with scrap wire and duct tape leaned against the walls. I didn't want to think about what else was contained in the layer of filth we were walking through.

Looking up, I spotted the hotel sign, a beacon of white-and-primary colors in the darkness—SMYLE. I smirked at the name, no feelings evoking a smile in that moment. Later that afternoon, when I discovered my international phone rates were astronomical and the walk to the hotel had cost us eighty dollars in data charges, I didn't care one bit. The price was worth the full collective breath we took once sequestered from the frenzy outside.

When we were settled, Ray and I determined our first order of business was to get local SIM cards for our phones.

"Do you guys want to come?" I asked RJ and Tyler, poking my head into their room.

"No. We'll just chill," Tyler said.

I hesitated but trusted they'd be fine. I didn't want to go back out, either.

Walking through the market, my senses were inundated, as if someone had turned up my sensitivity to maximum. The city was polluted, populous, and poverty-stricken. It hadn't rained in six months, and everything was coated with a thick layer of dust and dirt, giving the city an apocalyptic feel. Cars, motorcycles, and electric and human-powered tuk-tuks crammed bumper to bumper and side to side, all honking incessantly. Men coughed and attempted to clear their throats of the dust to the point of gagging themselves, then spat the offensive product on the street. They peed on the streets with no regard for who might be splattered by their urine. Half-starved, skeletal dogs wandered around, eating garbage. Cows roamed at their leisure, not looking much better than the dogs. The animals pooped everywhere. Women gathered cow patties and shaped them into flat, round cakes. Dried piles of these cakes lay stacked against buildings to be used for fuel. No one looked happy; faces displayed only scowls as people rushed through the market, pushing and shoving, elbows leading the way.

I kept my arm linked with Ray's so we wouldn't get separated as I tried to process my disappointment. Life seemed to require a constant reckoning between expectation and reality. *I should be used to that by now*, I thought.

We stopped at a store we thought sold SIM cards, but the clerk tried to lead us to another shop blocks from the main market. Once we realized his store was not "right around the corner," we turned around and ignored his protests. I was done being polite and apologetic, not taking ownership of my own direction. The next shop tried to sell us expired SIM cards at twice the printed price. When I questioned the clerk on the expiration date, he just shrugged as if he didn't care. Finally, we found a place that gave us a reasonable rate for two SIM cards and enough data to last the two weeks we'd planned to be in India.

Had India been our first stop on this trip, I'm not sure I would have continued. The amount of chaos would have triggered a panic attack at the start of the journey. I looked back now at being stuck in a parking lot in Okinawa and had to laugh. That experience was nothing compared to navigating the streets of Delhi.

We walked back to the hotel amid unfriendly stares, only disapproval on the faces in the crowd.

"It's as if everyone is sizing us up. Contemplating how to part us from whatever valuables we might have," I said.

Maybe being led astray only hours earlier contributed to my outlook, but I pulled myself a little closer to Ray, just in case I was right.

"Just stay aware of what's going on around us." Ray apparently didn't think my comments were too far off the mark.

Returning to the hotel, we checked in on RJ and Tyler and then returned to our room. I was deflated, ready to sleep and forget the day's trials.

Ray collapsed on the bed and closed his eyes. "Well, that was an adventure. What's in store for tomorrow?"

"We need to go to the Ghanaian embassy."

While searching for volunteer opportunities where Ray could provide dentistry and the boys and I could find activities and adventures to occupy our time, I discovered several organizations advertising volunteer opportunities, but the price tag attached ran anywhere from two thousand to five thousand dollars per person. This might have been a reasonable price for a two-week getaway, but was not a sustainable expense for long-term travel. While relaying this dilemma to a friend one day, she mentioned that she might be able to help. She arranged a meeting with a woman who lived part-time in our hometown of Bellingham and part-time in Ghana, Africa.

Ray and I met with Kathryn the summer before our departure. She told us of the organization she founded and ran in Cape Coast, that helped underprivileged students attend high school. Secondary school in Ghana was not free, and poor children did not have access to education beyond grade school without outside assistance.

"Why do you want to visit Ghana?" Kathryn asked during our visit.

I hadn't thought of going to Ghana specifically, but before I could answer, Ray chimed in. "I studied Ghana in school and always thought I'd like to visit."

His answer surprised me. I'd never heard him express a desire to see Ghana. Before embarking on our global adventure, I hadn't even known where Ghana was located. We had discussed going to Africa, but the only place we'd found where

Ray could volunteer was an isolated spot in Tanzania. With only a single building in a remote outpost, I wasn't sure what the boys and I would do to keep ourselves occupied for an extended period.

"I'm headed back to Ghana in a couple months," Kathryn said. "I'll see what I can find. There is a hospital in Cape Coast where I live that might take volunteers." She paused and looked at both of us pointedly. "But if I go to the trouble of finding a spot, I want to make sure you will follow through."

"If you find a place, we'll be there," Ray assured her.

True to her word, Kathryn e-mailed me shortly after her return to Ghana, having secured governmental approval for Ray to work at the Cape Coast University Hospital.

My next hurdle was to figure out how to get a Ghanaian visa while we were traveling. Visas typically required application within a fixed window and travel for a limited time period once approved. A Ghanaian visa had to be used within ninety days of issue. Since we weren't planning on visiting Ghana until six months into our trip, we weren't able to apply before leaving the US. And because we were always on the move as we traveled, we weren't able to send our passports back to the US embassy, since they were often required when checking into hotels and a necessity when moving between countries. We had chosen Delhi as a destination specifically because we needed to obtain visas while traveling. The Ghanaian embassy in Delhi seemed to be our best bet.

The next morning, we took a taxi to the embassy where we were dropped off at the front gates. I couldn't see the building behind the ten-foot concrete walls and reinforced steel gate, but guessed it must be a large complex, since the wall surrounded an entire city block. I walked up to the guard shack with the required paperwork in hand, expecting that we'd be ushered into the embassy, asked some questions, and approved for visas. After several calls to the main building, the guards indicated that we needed additional forms that weren't listed on the embassy's website.

No, we wouldn't be allowed inside to explain our case.

No, we were not of Indian descent.

No, they couldn't tell us what forms we were missing.

No, we couldn't talk to someone more knowledgeable.

I couldn't contain my frustration. My face turned red, as annoyance surged to a tipping point. I had done my home-work, followed all the rules. My irritation wasn't solely about not getting a visa. We'd promised Kathryn we would get to Ghana, and she had spent a great deal of time planning for us. We had an obligation to uphold, and I didn't want to let her down. But I wasn't about to start an argument with armed em-bassy guards who were already looking at me with suspicion. We would have to find a different way.

"I don't think they get many female American visitors," Ray said.

So much for The Force seeing us through that plan. Maybe the guards weren't familiar with *Star Wars*. Instead of a day at the embassy, we opted for a day of sight-seeing in Delhi.

Our first stop was Humayun's Tomb. The taxi driver pulled into a parking lot and pointed toward the entrance. Immediate-ly, we were surrounded by people begging for money and food. We'd encountered begging before on the trip, but this was a whole new level. People did not simply ask for money or food or stand on the street corners with signs asking for help. They followed us through the parking lot and across the street, poking our arms and backs until we were forced to pay atten-tion, if only to tell them to leave us alone. The beggars would then point to their mouths. Adults enlisted children to beg with practiced pouting faces and sad eyes. Even when we said *no*, we were followed for blocks and screamed at when we failed to acquiesce.

I watched my family's usual outgoing energy turn cold and impersonal. Tyler stopped smiling at people on the street, and RJ stayed close. He'd always had a sensitivity to unexpected touch, and I could sense his discomfort escalating.

"Why are they only begging from us?" Tyler asked.

"Look around, Ty. We're the only white people here," Ray said.

Before leaving, we'd talked about privilege and what it meant to be white in America, but this was a firsthand lesson.

I, too, was tired of being poked and saying *no*, but I wanted to explain more to the boys. "Even if we were the poorest white travelers, we would probably be considered wealthy here. I would guess the begging is largely due to the population in India and the competition for available resources. Maybe if the people don't fight to be first to get food or money, they starve to death."

Ray sensed the boys were getting it and continued the explanation. "India is a country with something like 1.3 billion people. In the United States, there are only around three hundred million. So, there are over four times as many people in a third of the space. Imagine if there were four families, sixteen people, living in our house but we only had enough food for four. We might think and behave a lot differently."

The boys looked around us at those begging in the crowds, studying them a little closer. I hoped they noticed the unwashed clothes, tangled hair, and dirty faces.

I was proud of our parenting in this moment but I couldn't help but reason that if India had been the first country we'd visited, we'd never have made it to a second. We'd made our way through increasingly complex situations, from an inescapable parking lot in Okinawa to a red-light district in Singapore, crossing the street in Vietnam to piloting e-bikes in Myanmar. I was happy I'd seen so much wonder before we'd encountered a darker side of travel. And I could see it wasn't only me who had changed, but Ray and the boys, too. We were all seeing the world through more educated eyes.

We collected touring lanyards and headphones after paying an entrance fee and entered the Humayun's Tomb complex. Recordings relayed information about the grounds and mausoleum—the first garden tomb on the Indian subcontinent and the first structure to use red sandstone on such a massive scale.

"Is this the Taj Mahal?" RJ asked.

"No," I said, though this structure seemed to be a replica of the Taj Mahal in red, even though Humayun's Tomb predated the Taj.

We took our time visiting the sixteenth-century buildings and gardens that surrounded the seventy-acre complex. I had relaxed in this compound, away from the intensity of the poverty and begging, and I could sense we were all avoiding going back out onto the city streets.

After a day of touring various monuments around Delhi, we returned to the market near our hotel and found a place for dinner. Worn out from the day's excursions, Ray looked at me and the boys in turn and asked, "Well . . . what do you think we should do next?" He poked at the chicken korma in front of him. I could tell he was not enjoying his meal.

"Well, since we're going to be in Nepal for a month, we'll have to send our passports back from there to the Ghanaian embassy in DC," I said. "If we can't figure it out, we won't be able to go to Ghana."

I'd been trying to work out the details of visas all day, prioritizing logistics. The sites were interesting, but I didn't feel the same connections I'd experienced elsewhere. My mind went back to the overarching dilemma. I didn't want to have to tell Kathryn we wouldn't make it to Ghana. The shame that came with disappointing someone still weighed heavy on me.

"Okay, but what about India?" Ray asked, dragging me back to the present.

"Well, I'd still love to see the Taj Mahal. We can look at how to get to Agra by train, and I think I saw a couple other places that looked interesting."

"Sounds good. But let's look at getting out to Rajasthan too. I really want to see the rats," Ray said.

We first heard of the rat temple at a travel lecture we'd attended the summer before our trip. A young man had taken a gap year to see the world before starting college. One of his stops was the Karni Mata "rat temple" in Rajasthan. I am not sure what made this temple stand out for Ray more than any other, but he never let go of the idea of traveling to this place.

I scrunched my face in disgust. "*Ew*. You really want to go there?"

The boys looked at Ray, trying to determine whether he was joking.

"It's something different. Something most people probably wouldn't do," he said. "Everyone gets a picture in front of the Taj Mahal."

I liked the idea of doing something different and the boys, too, seemed intrigued by the idea of an entire temple filled with rats. After dinner, we returned to the hotel and opened our laptops to plan our route to Agra. As we calculated the cost of hiring a car versus taking a train, Tyler came in our room and changed our plans in four words: "Mom, RJ is sick." We wouldn't be going anywhere for a while.

Evening gave way to night, and Ray continued to research while I watched over RJ, helping him to the bathroom, prepping cool cloths for his head, and trying to convince him to swallow some Tylenol. Ray was no help. Sick kids were not his department.

I sat next to RJ in one of the boys' two double beds and watched strange Indian movies, broken by even stranger commercials. Before long, Tyler was also racing for the bathroom and running a fever. As much as I didn't like to see my boys sick, I did like the closeness it brought, both boys allowing me to rub their backs and comb their hair with my fingers—gestures they'd avoid when well.

When I had the boys tucked in for the night, I walked next door to our room and found Ray curled up on the bathroom floor, unwilling to move to the bed. Fearing I might also take a turn at any moment, I checked in with my own body to gauge if I had any kind of discomfort or nausea. Nope, I was fine.

I had expected Ray would help the next day by running into the market for soda, crackers, and anything else we might want, but he was out of commission. This was on me. Just me. I tried to come up with a plan. I did a quick Google search to see what time it was in Montana, where my cousin, Jessie—a family physician and my on-call medical adviser during the trip—lived. Twelve-and-a-half-hour time difference. I wondered where the extra half hour came from, but wasn't interested enough to research further. Instead, I dug out the medical kit I'd prepared before the trip. I'd packed enough medications to see us around the world or at least cover us until we could find a doctor. Jessie had recommended bringing several different antibiotics, but I needed her advice to know whether this was an antibiotic-worthy issue.

By 7:00 p.m. India time, when I reasoned it was late enough in the morning in Montana, I phoned Jessie. She was happy to hear from me but knew something must be up for me to be calling from half a world away.

"What's wrong?" she asked.

"Ray and the boys are sick."

Jessie switched into doctor mode, her tone matter-of-fact. "What are their symptoms?"

I recounted all the gory details.

"Fevers?"

"Yes."

"Well, since you're in India, the most likely culprit is a bacterial infection from fecal contamination of the food," she said. "Start the antibiotics I gave you, the big white ones. Twice a day for five days. And if the boys aren't feeling better in forty-eight hours, get to a doctor."

"Will do. Thank you," I said.

"Hang in there and get everyone better. Love you," she said.

I was more at ease after the conversation. I hadn't realized just how worked up I'd been before I spoke with Jessie. Now that I'd been reassured antibiotics could get the boys back to normal, I realized I was exhausted from the tension I'd been holding onto.

"What'd she say?" Ray asked.

"Looks like you all have a bad case of Delhi-belly."

"That sounds a lot more fun than the reality of it." He laughed a little, and then moaned.

It was late December and the hotel had no heat, no towels, no bottled water, no housekeeping, and limited Wi-Fi. To compound the discomfort, everyone was too sick to move out of the budget hotel in "Slum Alley," as we'd begun to refer to the narrow passageway outside our temporary quarters.

Ray and the boys tried to sleep between trips to the bathroom. For several days, I marched down the alley, holding my breath as I passed the two open urinals on the way to the main street, ignoring the poking and sleeve-tugging along the way. I found a market and bought soda and whatever could stand in for saltine crackers. Back at the hotel, I spent my days taking temperatures, dishing out antibiotics, and generally trying to nurse all my boys back to health.

Waking up one morning to the sound of men outside in the alleyway hacking, coughing, and spitting, almost to the point of vomiting themselves, I glanced at my watch: 6:34 a.m., December 25. I had forgotten, or maybe I'd tried to forget, it was Christmas.

"Merry Christmas," I said, the hacking outside provoking my own gag reflex.

"This is the worst Christmas ever," Ray said. "We've got to get out of here."

I had to agree. But, although concerned for Ray and the boys, I felt lighter than I had in years. This was temporary. I would take Christmas in a backpacker ghetto hotel with all my boys sick over The Glitch any time.

Agra

After a few days, when Ray and the boys were feeling almost back to normal, we resumed our conversation about how to spend our remaining days in India. Although our attempt at Ghanaian visas and getting sick had used up several days, our flight to Nepal wasn't scheduled for another week. Everyone wanted to get out of "Slum Alley." RJ and I still wanted to see the Taj Mahal, and Ray and Tyler agreed that an off-the-wall adventure to a rat temple sounded interesting.

"There is no way you and the boys are going to be up for the crowds if we travel by train." I knew it would be more expensive to travel by car, but the Dailey health meter was running low, and my instincts told me we'd be miserable facing the crowded train stations. "And I think we need a little more control over bathroom stops."

"Let's hire a guide," Ray said in agreement. "That will be our Christmas present to ourselves."

The hotel arranged the trip from their one-room tour office—possibly a former janitorial closet. We packed our bags and left on a week-long excursion around India's famed Golden Triangle—a tourist circuit connecting Delhi to Agra and Jaipur. The first leg of the journey took us to the Taj Mahal, a hundred and forty miles away. With all that had gone wrong, I still hoped the India I'd fallen in love with from books I'd read was out there. I still believed I could find the good India had to offer. I knew my family to be open-hearted travelers and I didn't want the assault on our senses and bodies to close us down.

During our drive to Agra, I stared out the window at factory upon factory, each with a smokestack belching a toxic, low-lying brown cloud over the land. The factories churned out mud bricks to build houses for the ever-increasing population of the country.

Passing a dead cow on the side of the road, I glanced at the boys to see if they'd noticed. Deep in conversation about Minecraft formulas, they hadn't seen it. A few minutes later, however, they didn't miss a livestock truck full of dead, bloated cow carcasses passing in the other direction. Despite the closed windows and blasting air conditioning, we all got a long whiff of putrid stink. Rolling down the windows didn't dissipate the smell; this was one stench we had to suffer through. I assumed the animals were being taken to be buried or burned.

Nearing the city, Tyler pointed to a man on the side of the road. "Mom, look, that guy is naked."

His dark skin was covered in a dingy white paint, giving him an ashy look, as if he'd just rolled around in a fire pit. His matted gray hair and beard hung midway down his torso. His forehead was marked with white, red, and yellow paint, and his neck was strung with beads. But his only clothing consisted of a brown string tied around his waist.

"Uh, yep. He sure is," I replied.

"Why is he naked?" Ray asked our driver.

"He is Sadhu," the driver replied, either thinking that was explanation enough or maxing out the extent of his English skills.

Later that evening, I read that Sadhu were men on a pilgrimage. They typically walked along roads with begging bowls and staffs and were given food in return for their blessings and prayers. Severing ties with family was expected, and Sadhu wore markings and clothes associated with the sect they belonged to. Sadhus occupied a position roughly equal to that of domestic servants. Most gave up affiliation with caste and kin and underwent a funeral ceremony for themselves, followed by a ritual rebirth into their new life, at which time they also renounced all worldly possessions—including clothing.

Many Sadhu were making their way to Agra. Nearing the city, the sight of a solo, naked man—and sometimes a group of naked men—ambling along the road became common.

After navigating our way through the gridlocked traffic for hours, we ended up at a guesthouse in the late afternoon. The young man who checked us in recommended dinner at a rooftop café where we'd have a sunset view of the Taj Mahal. The luminous white monument was packed with people, and I was struck first with a sense of awe, and then dread at dealing with crowds with my barely healthy crew.

When our waiter approached, I asked, "Is it always that crowded?"

"No," he said. "Today is a holy day. People come from very far to visit the tomb and pay homage to love."

That explained the traffic and frequency of Sadhu.

After dinner, we walked back to our guesthouse along quiet streets under a sky stained pink by the setting sun and haze. Our pace was unhurried, and I was proud of the travelers we'd become. During The Glitch, it seemed impossible that I would ever feel anything but grief. But here in India, halfway around the world from home, even with the unexpected detours and sickness, my sadness was dissolving.

Arriving at the Taj Mahal early the next morning, I was disappointed to see a line winding around the corner. As we searched for the end, guards pointed us to a separate entrance for tourists which had no line at all. Even though we benefited, I felt a sense of unfairness, like we were cheating the system.

The Taj Mahal grounds were immaculate. Although visitors threw garbage wherever they pleased, ignoring the trash receptacles lining the walkways, crews cleaned nonstop. At the placard near the entrance, we read that the Taj Mahal, meaning "Crown of the Palaces" was commissioned in 1632 by the Mughal emperor, Shah Jahan, to house the tomb of his favorite wife, Mumtaz Mahal, a Persian princess who died giving birth to their fourteenth child. I knew the Taj Mahal was an homage to love, but I hadn't known the story behind the structure, and I was surprised to learn its age. The date of construction made me appreciate the beauty of this marble mausoleum even more than I had before.

"I expect you to commission something on this scale when I die," Ray said.

"Only after you birth fourteen children." I gave Ray a sly smile.

The morning sun shone bright in a cloudless sky, and I found it difficult to keep my eyes open against the reflection off the brilliant white building. Nearing the tomb, we found the grounds strewn with piles of shoes—footwear was not allowed to touch any part of the white marble. And just as we did at the main entrance, we found another long line snaking down the path, everyone waiting in bare feet to climb the stairs to the main platform. Once again, the line was only for Indians, and we were directed to an entrance without any line. We skipped the shoe rack too, as tourists were not required to remove shoes, but simply cover them with fabric booties.

I thought climbing the stairs and standing on the platform outside the central building would be the extent we'd be allowed to explore, but entering and visiting the tomb itself was permitted. The flow of traffic crept through a single doorway, one line going in and another coming out. An armed guard stood on duty, ensuring the flow continued. We were pushed and shoved toward the tomb of Shah Jahan and his wife Mumtaz Mahal in the center of the monument.

I stared for my allotted thirty seconds at the fake coffins—the sarcophagi were false, the real ones not available for viewing—feeling changed by India, but not in the way I had anticipated or wanted. India had knocked us down with sickness and challenged my optimism. As much as I'd been resistant to the idea of returning home, I had to admit home now seemed to be calling my name, at least in whispers.

When we reconnected with our driver after our Taj visit, Ray took him aside, pulled out a map, and said, "We don't want to continue on the trip around the Golden Triangle. Too many people. We would like to go to Bikaner in Rajasthan. I know the tour office said no, but what do you think?"

"Bikaner? Okay," the driver replied.

Ray got into the car and relayed the verdict. "Okay, I think we're heading to Rajasthan."

"That was easy." When Ray and I discussed a change in plans, I thought it would be much more difficult to convince the driver. "Are you sure he understood?"

"I think so," Ray replied.

"He's probably tired of all the people, too," Ty said.

Bikaner

Towns spread out and the population dwindled the closer we got to Bikaner—a town in the middle of the Thar Desert, seventy miles away from the Pakistan border. India and Pakistan had a tenuous relationship and had engaged in numerous military conflicts. Due to the political unrest and perceived danger, we kept our proximity to Pakistan to ourselves when corresponding with home. Although I was relieved to have some distance from the crowds of Delhi and Agra, I had to admit that being so close to Pakistan made me nervous.

The next morning, we asked our driver to make the Karni Mata Temple our first stop. Karni Mata was a female Hindu sage who, according to a legend from the fifteenth century, pleaded with the God of Death to bring her nephew back to life after he drowned in a pond. The God refused at first, but eventually relented, saying all Karni Mata's relations would be reincarnated—as rats. As painful as it had been to lose so many family members during The Glitch, I was quite certain I wouldn't want them reincarnated as rats.

At first glance, the exterior of the temple wasn't what I was expecting. We stared at a twenty-foot Pepto-pink wall surrounding an open courtyard.

"What are they selling?" RJ asked, pointing to vendors near the entrance.

I walked up to a vendor to find out.

"Would you like food for the rats?" he asked.

I hadn't anticipated feeding the rodents, but the vendor persisted.

"You will have good fortune if you eat food that has been nibbled on by kabbas," he said.

"What are kabbas?" RJ asked.

"The holy rats are called kabbas," the vendor said. "You will also have good fortune if the rats touch your feet or if you see the white rat."

At that point I noticed a stand near the entrance for storing shoes, because, as in many of the temples in Asia, shoes were not allowed. The thought of rats scampering over my bare feet and the filth I'd be walking through made me shiver. I knew I wouldn't be nibbling on anything that had been gnawed on by a rat, but I purchased a bag of food for the boys to feed to the critters.

We deposited our footwear at the shoe stand and entered the arena. Small rooms ringed the courtyard in the temple's interior space, each housing a different Hindu shrine. Karni Mata devotees served grain and milk from large metal bowls to some twenty thousand rats. The downside to having all these creatures in one place, fighting and nibbling on sweets all day, was that the rats were prone to disease. Stomach disorders and diabetes in the rodent population were common, and every few years an epidemic ran rampant and decimated their numbers.

That didn't stop my family. While I tried not to scream every time a rat scurried over my feet, Ray and the boys competed to see who could attract the most rats. It didn't take long for them to have a swarm of critters vying for the food pellets from their outstretched hands. But when the rats started mistaking their fingers for food and taking little test nibbles, the game ended.

Walking through the dark rooms with glowing shrines, I kept my eye out for the mysterious white rat. Occasionally, a small commotion would erupt with people racing to one room or another when a yelp attracted their attention. I suspected the yelps were a reaction to rats nibbling on toes rather than a glimpse of this good luck charm. The only white I saw in the temple came from the shallow metal bowls of milk encircled by a throng of long-tailed varmints.

Returning to the shoe stand after our visit, we brushed off the bottom of our now blackened feet as best as we could before slipping on socks and shoes.

"Well, you got us to the rat temple," I said to Ray, gagging a little at the thought of rat droppings now being ground into my socks and shoes. "What are you going to do with us next? Sneak us into Pakistan just for kicks?"

"Maybe, but let's go by camel," Ray quipped.

"Camel?"

"Sure, why not? When in the desert . . . ."

After a day of wandering around Bikaner and visiting the sixteenth-century Junagarh Fort—a huge complex of ornate halls and the main tourist attraction in this small town—our driver dropped us off on the side of the road where a group of camels and young men waited for us. The day before, Ray had seen an advertisement for a camel safari in the hotel lobby.

We met our guides and were given a brief lesson on mounting these long-limbed animals. The camels sat in a neat row, their legs bent underneath their bodies, each dusty animal with a handler crouched near its head. Getting on a camel was not unlike mounting a horse . . . at first. Once we were each situated in a saddle, the guide told us to hang on tight. One by one, the six-foot-tall animals stood by extending their back legs first, lurching us forward toward their heads, then pitching us back as they extended their front legs to stand fully. I let out a squeal, clinging to the saddle as tight as I could to prevent a six-foot fall to the ground.

Atop these giant ships of the desert, there wasn't much to do but relax into the sway and admire our surroundings. Rolling hills covered with sand and pocked with desiccated scrub brush and scraggly trees surrounded us in every direction. The evening sun lengthened our shadows so we looked like alien beings on stilt-legged steeds. The young handlers led the camels along a dusty path toward our destination. Typically, this adventure would end at a camp five miles into the dessert where tourists could spend the night and ride back out the next morning. However, December in India was chilly, with temperatures reaching no more than seventy degrees Fahrenheit during the day and dipping into the forties at night. We opted to ride camels to the camp, have dinner, then take a Jeep back to the starting point after dark.

Lumbering along, RJ and Tyler started snickering, each making the other laugh harder.

"What's going on back there? What's so funny?" I asked.

"The camels are farting," RJ said, trying to catch his breath.

"A lot," Tyler added, the laughter starting again.

I laughed along with them, happy to be at the front of the caravan.

An hour later, when the sun dipped behind the hills and the pink sky turned a deep purple-blue, our camels deposited us at the camp where a whole crew awaited our arrival. One man handed out hot towels to wipe the dust from our faces. Another poured a shot of rum to warm our insides.

"What's this?" Ray asked, as he took a small sip from the glass.

"Indian rum, very good," replied our guide.

"It was really good, Dad," Ty said and RJ nodded his agreement, both boys having downed their shot in one gulp.

We relaxed with drinks around a large fire, where we were serenaded with traditional Rajasthan folk music. Two men sat cross-legged on a blanket, one beating rhythm on a drum, the second running his bow across the *tar shehnai*—a stringed instrument with bells along the neck—its notes amplified by a metal horn attached to the base. Both musicians sang along, their voices and the *tar shehnai* somewhat discordant to our ears. After a few songs, the musicians asked about our musical abilities. When Tyler admitted he played the bass clarinet, they convinced him to try his hand at playing the *tar shehnai*, the notes he produced equally inharmonious.

After the fireside concert, the guide led us to a table where we were served a five-course meal under the stars. I wrapped my lap blanket a little tighter to keep out the chill and looked up at the glittering night sky. I had finally found some peace in India, a tiny slice of the beauty the stories had promised.

I laughed to myself thinking about how twenty thousand rats and farting camels had become the highlight of our India adventure. I had really wanted to love India. Knowing I would be entering a country of chaos, I anticipated falling in love with the colors, sights, sounds, smells, people, places—a bustling world so different from my own. But I would have to settle for taking the gift India had given me, which was to understand and harness my own power. I could be relied upon when my family needed me. I had the ability to solve problems and change direction, flowing with the stream rather than fighting against it. India turned out to be "level ten" on the travel game scale but it had not beaten us. We still had lives left to play and many levels to explore.

Days of Travel: 129
Miles Logged: 24,084

HARMONY AMID CHAOS

Kathmandu, Nepal

Some places on Earth—like Delhi—reveal the unpleasantries in the state of the world, highlight the dichotomy between thought and action, cause your chest to ache so hard at the state of the human condition you think it will explode. Other places invite you to breathe, to be peaceful, to connect to yourself. Much to my relief, Nepal was the latter. Everything about Nepal felt like the opposite of what we'd experienced in India. From the visa process to walking through the city to the people, even the air quality itself—everything improved when we left India.

In a cruel twist of fate, however, the people of Nepal were living in the Dark Ages compared to their neighboring country. For more than a decade, the country had been subject to load-shedding—a process aimed at removing load from the power grid through a system of planned, rolling blackouts—essentially forced conservation. Though this happens periodically in both developed and developing nations when demand exceeds capacity, during the dry winter months in Nepal, homes received electricity for as little as two hours per day.

Due to a political dispute with India during the time of our visit, the Indian government blocked fuel trucks from crossing the border into Nepal, thus adding a fuel crisis to the country's energy demands.

We spent our first few days in the capital city of Kathmandu. In April of the prior year, a magnitude 7.8 earthquake killed nine thousand people in Nepal, injured many more, and damaged or destroyed more than six hundred thousand structures in Kathmandu and nearby towns. The earthquake also cut off many remote villages due to impassable roadways. Evidence of the earthquake was everywhere. Many buildings had been reduced to piles of bricks yet to be cleared or rebuilt. Monuments once frequented by locals and tourists alike displayed gaping cracks and were closed until further notice.

The people of the city did not seem to wallow in their misfortune. Prayer flags and colorful streamers fluttered back and forth above the streets, bringing a lightness and joy to the area. Streets were swept clean each day, and we were met with smiles and the greeting "Namaste," complete with hands together in a prayer and heads bowed. I fell in love with this recovering city instantly.

After enjoying a few days in Kathmandu, we arranged for a taxi to take us to the town of Dhulikhel where Ray would work at the dental hospital for a month. With sixteen thousand residents, Dhulikhel was tiny compared to Kathmandu's population of over a million. The journey of thirty miles took ninety minutes as we wound up and down the foothills of the Himalayas, through smaller towns and villages. While the slow pace could have been frustrating, I relaxed into the journey, having been calmed by the pace of the country and easygoing manner of the people.

Watching the city pass by as we drove, we noticed long lines of cars at each gas station we passed.

"Where are the owners?" Ray asked our driver.

"Sometimes we have to wait two days for gas," he said. "So people park cars and wait at home until a gas truck comes in. People take turns and make calls to their friends when the truck arrives."

Our hotel in Kathmandu had a generator providing power throughout the day, but we knew in Dhulikhel this would not be the case.

"What do you do about power? Does it go on at the same time every day?" I asked.

"No, it is different every day and there is no pattern. At least not one anyone can figure out. But there is an app you can download for your phone. It will give you the day's schedule for the zone you're in."

I pulled my phone out of my pocket and began my search for the load-shedding schedule.

"How do people get to work and school?" Ray asked.

"We do the best we can."

Along our drive to Dhulikhel, we passed buses crammed full of people. So full that local laws had been suspended and people were allowed to ride on top of the bus. Even in the chill January air, people climbed the ladder at the rear of the bus and huddled together against the wind, a small luggage bar the only thing keeping them from sliding to the ground.

"We are also still suffering aftershocks from last year's earthquake," the driver added.

"Really? Are they bad?" asked Ray.

"No, but there are a lot. There is an app for earthquakes, too, so you can see how big they are and where they hit," he answered. It seemed incongruous to me for a country in so much turmoil to have apps for power schedules and earthquakes, much like the first time I saw a monk take a picture with his cell phone.

Dhulikhel

Once in Dhulikhel, we were directed up a steep hill to a three-story, cinder-block guesthouse. The hospital ran the guesthouse to accommodate the constant rotation of visiting medical students and instructors. Each of the nine rooms in the building was furnished with two single beds, a small shelf, and, occasionally, a desk. No TV, coffeemaker, or single-serve toiletries you'd find in western accommodations. Ray and I were lucky to claim a room with an attached toilet and sink, but there was only one shower for everyone in the entire building. Hot water was supplied through an on-demand water heater hooked up to a propane tank in a fifty-gallon drum in the hallway.

In January, temperatures ranged from thirty-five to sixty-five degrees. While these temperatures were not terribly different from a Pacific Northwest spring season, there was no heating system in the guesthouse. Even if there had been a heating system, it would have required power or gas, of which there was little to go around. Compared to our room—a consistent forty-five to fifty degrees—Tyler and RJ's room received sunshine for much of the day, warming it considerably. We spent indoor time in their room doing homework and playing games.

I wondered how the boys and I would get through the hours of the day without power and nothing to keep us occupied in this small town. But our days in Dhulikhel fell into a comfortable routine. Ray woke each morning, climbed two floors to the rooftop kitchen and ate breakfast with the other medical students and instructors before walking a mile to the hospital. Once the boys were awake, the three of us climbed to the roof and ate our breakfast of fresh bread, homemade yogurt, a hard-boiled egg, and milk tea. Most days, I helped the boys get through some schoolwork, although this had become more of a way to spend some empty hours rather than get caught up. At the outset of the trip, I worried about whether missing a year of school would set them back in their lives, but this worry, like so many others, had faded. We had no official plan for their missed school time and would deal with the consequences when we returned.

Although the guesthouse provided breakfast and dinner, for lunch we were on our own. Between subjects, as hunger pangs began, the boys and I walked the mile into town for lunch, down one hill and up another. Flat areas were rare in Dhulikhel; the town was built on a terraced landscape in the foothills of the Himalayas. Our favorite lunch was momos— little dough pockets filled with either chicken, buffalo, or veggies. We sat in a cold, dark café, lit only by the sunlight coming in the windows, and waited as food was cooked, one meal at a time, over an outdoor fire pit. We became accustomed to the leisurely pace and extended meals. I began to see the uninterrupted time spent with my boys as an opportunity to connect with them, reflect on the favorite parts of our adventure and what was still to come.

Often the boys and I walked through the narrow streets of "old town" and visited the many temples built in the middle of cobblestone streets. Walking also helped generate heat in our bodies. RJ took to the culture immediately. He greeted everyone we encountered with palms pressed together, a slight head bow, saying "Namaste" with a wide smile, which was always reciprocated with a similar greeting.

With little electronic distraction, no chores to attend to, and only ourselves to entertain, the boys and I were free to wander, explore, and appreciate the small town we called home for a short while. This was an in-between time where we could just be. We began to appreciate the quiet simplicity of each day, spending time together, lingering over lunch, finishing a book in one sitting, glimpses of the snowcapped Himalayas, a trail of caterpillars along the road, even peanut butter—a rare find in most of Asia, but something carried in the local grocery store.

On Saturdays—the only day Ray didn't work at the clinic—we'd start our morning with banana pancakes, chocolate French toast, and coffee at a little place in the middle of town called Nawaranga Guesthouse and Art Gallery. The owner was a charming older man who took great pride in his family-owned establishment and support of local artists. After delivering our meals, he sat with us as we ate and told stories about Nepal.

One weekend, after our pancake breakfast, we scaled the thousand steps to Kali Temple, just outside of town. At the top of the hill, we climbed a three-story tower to get a better view of the valley, far below. Had the sky been clear, we would have been able to see the Himalayas, but due to the power shortage, many homes in Nepal relied on wood fires, and smoke clogged the valley.

On the evenings when the smoke was light and the sky was clear, Ray and I would watch the blue turn to pink and marvel at the steep mountains from our seats on the rooftop. We were mesmerized by the Himalayas in the distance glowing in the setting sun.

"Have you figured out what to do about Ghana visas?" Ray asked during one rooftop session.

I had taken on the job of trying to figure out how to finish this task.

I raised my glasses to the top of my head and rubbed my eyes, tired from my endless searching on the computer that day. "I've looked at all the possibilities I can think of. And it's going to be more complicated than I imagined."

"More complicated than sending our passports to the US and hoping they make it back to us?" Ray asked.

I nodded. "Yeah, there are a lot of moving parts. First, I have to send all the paperwork along with our passports to your mom. She will need to add a cashier's check to the items and then FedEx that package to the embassy in DC, along with a second FedEx envelope addressed to us here."

"Wait," Ray interrupted. "Why does she have to add a check? Can't we pay with a credit card and send them directly to the embassy from here?"

"Nope. Has to be a cashier's check in US funds, which I can't get in Nepal." I looked out to the snow-capped mountains—such calm compared to the intricacies of bureaucracy. "I tried two different banks today and even met with the manager. So, your mom will add the check, and then forward the package to the embassy. Once the embassy does their thing, they'll FedEx our passports, with visas, back here to Nepal."

"Sounds like you have it all figured out. Is there more to it?" Ray never ceased to amaze me with his easy acceptance.

"Well, just one thing. I have to go back into Kathmandu to send the package. That's the closest FedEx office. I checked in town where we saw a FedEx sign, but they only accept deliveries, and the post office won't do it, either." I sat back in my chair and looked at Ray. "And we could run into some problems. I don't know for sure that the embassy will send the passports back to us in Nepal. But even if they do, it could take up to ten days for them to process our applications. This all has to happen in a short time frame, because our thirty-day visas here will be up in a couple of weeks."

"I think we'll be okay if we have to stay here longer," Ray said.

"If the timing works in our favor, even allowing the embassy a week for processing, we should have our documents back here the day before we're scheduled to leave," I said.

"And if we don't get the visas?" Ray asked.

"I haven't looked into the consequences yet. But if the embassy won't send them back to Nepal, I guess we'll just have to figure it out." I paused and let logic, rather than panic, dictate my next words. "I suspect they'd send the package back to our home address, which would then have to be sent back here. And if nothing works out as planned, we find a US embassy to help us get back to the States without our passports." I shrugged, then smiled at Ray to let him know I was doing okay. "But I don't think it will come to that."

Ray looked at me, eyebrows raised in question.

"Really. I actually think everything will work out fine."

I felt confident about the steps that would get us to our next destination. The easy pace of Dhulikhel had allowed me the time and focus to work through all the options. Even if the plan didn't work, I wasn't worried about being in Nepal without documentation like I might have been elsewhere. Especially in this small town, I didn't believe anyone would demand to see my passport. The return to confidence and effective problem-solving was empowering. This is what I knew I was good at—maneuvering my way through problems to get to a solution.

"Okay. When are you going to go to Kathmandu?" Ray asked.

"The boys and I will go tomorrow. Meen said he'd arrange for a driver to take us there and back."

Meen was a young man who ran the guesthouse and cooked breakfast and dinner for all the visitors. Though finding a taxi in Dhulikhel was difficult, Meen was from the area and knew everyone, making finding and hiring a car easy.

"See if you can pick up a small space heater while you're there. We can at least warm our room a little when there's power," Ray said.

We took one last look at the now-darkening sky and joined the rest of the guests in the one-room kitchen. Our family of four gathered around a large table with the other guests, where we ate dinner by oil lamp and solar-powered lantern. Conversation centered around the happenings of the day, whether anyone felt aftershocks, and the outreaches around Nepal. We learned that the hospital put together medical and dental teams to visit isolated villages cut off after the earthquake and many of the students and instructors here had taken part in one of the missions. Since none of us were from Nepal, we also traded travel stories. There was a camaraderie among this group of foreigners who all appreciated the welcoming spirit of Nepal, astounded by the fortitude of the people living with so little.

The next morning after Ray left for work, the boys and I took a taxi back to Kathmandu. I arranged to meet up with our driver at noon, giving me an hour to get our paperwork mailed to the US and allowing the boys and me a little time to shop for a space heater and treats at a market. I didn't give a second thought to roaming around in a foreign country without our passports. Once I'd sent them off, there wasn't much I could do about it, anyway. I had to trust The Force.

Back at the guesthouse that night during dinner, Ray announced he'd been asked to accompany the dental team on an outreach.

As Ray and I were discussing the details and how long he'd be gone, Meen said to me, "Why don't you and the boys go on a trek while Ray is gone?"

"A trek?" I asked, not hiding my unease.

A trek sounded like more than I was prepared for, physically or mentally. I pictured people wrapped in parkas, fur-lined gloves, face masks and goggles donning oxygen tanks and battling their way up waist-high snow drifts in a quest to reach the summit of the tallest mountain on Earth. I was in the Himalayas after all.

"There is a small village about fifteen kilometers from here called Namo Buddha," Meen said. "I can call the resort and let them know you are coming. They will have a room prepared and will arrange for dinner and breakfast the next morning. You only need a small pack with clothes, and I'll pack snacks for the hike."

"You guys should go," Ray said.

The thought of trekking alone with my boys in a foreign country without Ray intimidated me, until some of the students who had done the same trek chimed in and raved about the beauty of the scenery along the trail. I did a quick calculation in my head—fifteen kilometers . . . not quite ten miles—and decided I was up for the adventure. I had to smile. The more I thought about the trek, the more excited I became.

I turned to RJ and Tyler. "What do you guys think?" I wanted some buy-in from the boys, too.

"Sure, let's go," Ty said.

RJ nodded agreement.

"Okay, Meen," I said. "Point us in the right direction."

Namo Buddha

When the day arrived, Ray and I said goodbye, our hug lingering, both of us knowing we would not be able to communicate until we all returned to the guesthouse in a few days. We had barely been apart for months, and I had come to rely on our closeness, our shared decision-making and planning, but this felt like the right time to step out on my own.

"Have a great time," he said. "You'll be fine."

I nodded. "We will be fine as long as we don't get lost."

"And stop looking at that earthquake app," Ray added, over his shoulder.

He knew me too well. I'd been checking for aftershocks several times a day. There had been many since we arrived, but I'd never felt one.

Shortly after breakfast, the boys and I took a now familiar trail, again tackling the thousand stairs to Kali Temple. Following the trail further, we found wooden signs with faded lettering pointing the way to Namo Buddha. Along the dusty path, we passed houses in all states of disrepair. Homes constructed of dried mud and sticks had been so damaged by the earthquake and aftershocks that, in many cases, entire walls were still missing from the structures.

As we passed houses with young children, they ran to the edge of their property shouting, "Chocolate?" Meen told us before we left that trekkers hiking through the villages of Nepal and up into the mountains used to carry chocolate and pass it out to children along the way. The practice had long since been discouraged, although not entirely forgotten. The boys and I would shake our heads apologetically and wave as we passed, hoping a smile and a "Namaste" would suffice. The children smiled back, waving us on our way.

We continued along the terraced landscape covered in a blanket of small yellow wildflowers. We climbed for long stretches, often catching views of the snow-covered Himalayas to our left. Prayer flags were strung from tree to tree across the path, like they were in the streets of Kathmandu. The only sound was the fall of our footsteps and the rustling of the trees. The flags swayed in the light breeze, some bright yellow, red, blue, and green, others so sun-faded their original color was indistinct. The flags imparted a sense of calm and serenity, as if Buddha were watching over us. I was reminded of being in the shadow of the stupas in Myanmar. Could it be true that by simply standing in their presence, calm was restored? I decided it was.

While there was only seven hundred and fifty feet of elevation difference between Dhulikhel and Namo Buddha, the trekking route took us up and down the many hills between the two villages.

We made two minor wrong turns but were set straight with the help of kind people along the path. By early afternoon, we arrived at our destination. Ingrid, a middle-aged German woman who owned the resort, welcomed us. After checking us in and calling for lunch to be prepared, she served hot tea and sat with us on the patio. Several cats prowled around seeking our attention, which the boys were more than happy to provide. From the patio we had views stretching to the north and south, even to the Himalayas—less than seventy miles away.

"Meen told us you suffered heavy damage in the earthquake. Has the resort recovered?" I asked Ingrid.

"The damage was quite bad at first. We all were sleeping outside in makeshift tents, afraid to sleep in the houses with all the shaking. Even though it was rainy and cold, no one knew the extent of the damage and didn't want to risk being crushed." Ingrid gestured toward an open area of land where a large, makeshift structure constructed of little more than wooden poles covered with plastic tarps still stood. "Tourism took a big hit. The resort directly supported about thirty-five families, and I couldn't keep all my employees. But now things are improving. Most of our cottages have been repaired and our garden is back in working order. Right now, we are closed, but we expect to have all the cottages ready when we open in late February."

"You're closed?" I asked, surprised by this statement.

"Yes, but we have guests that come through from time to time, like you," she said, smiling.

"Thank you for having us."

Sitting in the sun, I had a realization, again, of the importance of taking opportunities when life presented them.

Ingrid joined us for lunch and continued to tell us about the area. She and her husband had built the resort to create a sustainable business that would last for generations. They grew as much of their food as possible, including vegetables, grains, and fruits to use in their strictly vegetarian menu. The kitchen staff made fresh sourdough bread and collected milk from buffalo daily to make cheese and ice cream. When they needed to supplement, they purchased from local farmers to support the surrounding economy. The staff at the resort were from neighboring villages and not trained in tourism, but willing to learn. Together they created an authentic experience for travelers. Even the bed cushions and linens were handwoven and designed with traditional Nepalese patterns.

After lunch, I had visions of a short rest and a hot shower. Meen had mentioned that the resort had a generator, so hot water and heat were available all day. Ingrid had other plans for us, however.

"You should walk over to the monastery for evening prayers," she said, before I could ask. "It's a beautiful place to visit and they will serve you bread and tea. When you return, you will have time to rest before dinner at seven."

"Is it okay for us to watch their ceremony?" I felt like we would be intruding on something sacred, something private.

"Oh, yes. There are always people who watch. We often walk over. It's an amazing experience," she replied. "I'm sure you'll see other travelers there, too."

We said goodbye to the cats—one of which was nestled, purring in RJ's lap—and hiked the two miles to the monastery, once again up and down the terraced landscape. Walking up a winding road to an enormous complex on top of a hill, we didn't notice any other tourists. In fact, we didn't see anyone on the grounds at all. Surrounded by mountains and now large buildings, we were alone.

"Is this the place?" RJ asked. He, too, had noticed we were the only people walking toward the monastery.

"This has to be it. It's the only building around here," I said.

The trail Ingrid had directed us to led only one way.

"Mom, let's turn around," Tyler said.

I glanced at him and could tell he felt out of place and was worrying about not seeing anyone.

With a reassuring tone, I said, "No, let's go a little farther. I'm not ready to give up quite yet."

I knew what Tyler was feeling all too well; I'd let it control me too often. I wasn't afraid to make a mistake anymore. I wanted to demonstrate to my boys that not achieving the intended outcome was okay.

We wandered further into the complex and began to see an occasional robed figure walking toward a building in the center.

"That must be where we're supposed to go. C'mon," I said, heading toward the same building.

"Mom, how do you know?" Tyler asked.

"I don't know for sure, but let's find out," I said, trusting we were in the right place, even if it was the wrong place.

I smiled to myself. I was confident, able to move beyond my own worries, perhaps returning to the woman Ray had never lost sight of and continued to urge to return.

We walked into the entryway and at once noticed an area filled with shoes, but no people. A small sign asked for shoes and socks to be removed.

"This is the place," I said, giving Tyler a reassuring smile.

"How do you know?" he asked.

I pointed to the pile of shoes in front of us. "Look at those shoes, Ty. *Columbia, Merrell, Nike.* I don't think this is monks' footwear."

We removed our dusty socks and shoes, each of us noting the line of grime we'd accumulated on our trek. I led the way up a flight of stairs, the cold marble making my bare toes ache. I could hear instruments being tuned. When we arrived at the entrance to the large room, a monk greeted us silently with palms pressed together and a small bow, but this time, no words. We reciprocated the greeting and followed him to pillows set along the wall, where he extended his hand and invited us to sit. As my eyes adjusted to the dim lighting, I noticed there were several other groups of onlookers seated near us. I gave Tyler a little nudge to make sure he also saw them.

"I just feel really uncomfortable, Mom," Ty said, after the monk had set a small table in front of our pillows.

I heard a familiar ring of anxiety in Tyler's voice, reminding me of myself in similar moments. I knew this was a moment in which I could either confirm his uneasiness or demonstrate how to move beyond the anxiety.

"I know, hon', but we're okay. Ingrid assured us we're welcome here. Let's see what happens," I said.

We saw other foreigners seated around the perimeter and several more people appeared after we were seated, surprising since we hadn't seen anyone on the walk. We watched as monks entered the dimly lit room and sat down at long tables stretching the entire length of the room. Some monks held instruments, others carried trays of cakes. Several monks in their saffron robes served warm milk tea to the guests, followed by slices of sweet bread. When the guests had been served, the process continued until the monks had had their share of tea and cake. Once everyone had eaten, the monks played a variety of instruments and chanted. The beating of large drums and bellowing of conch shells made a deep, resonating sound that vibrated through my body.

I glanced over at Ty. He seemed to be less anxious and was now interested in the ceremony, so I closed my eyes and let my body relax. My breath synced to the rhythm of the music. For a moment, I was sad Ray was not here to enjoy the experience, but I was also proud of myself for not giving up on this adventure.

After the ceremony, we hiked back to the resort as the sun disappeared behind the hills and the stars began to shine.

Days of Travel: 154
Miles Logged: 24,843

FEAR OF RETURN

Cape Coast, Ghana

Four days before I'd predicted, our passports arrived by Fed-
Ex, complete with visas. We were finally on our way to Ghana.

"Wow, look out there," I said, pressing my forehead against
the airplane's window, trying to take in as much of the landscape as I could.

We had just crossed over the Mediterranean Sea and were
flying above the Sahara Desert.

"It's so beautiful," Tyler said.

At sunset, the pinks and reds of the sky, combined with the
flowing patterns in the sand, left us all in quiet awe. Who knew
how many thousands of years or windstorms it had taken for
natural forces to form this ocean of sand, sweeping the dunes
into undulating patterns that held the eye? I knew one thing
for certain as I looked down at the desert below us—even in
this desolate landscape, change was inevitable. There was no
stopping it.

Once we landed in Accra, we gathered luggage and hired a
taxi to take us to the hotel. I was so relieved we'd finally made it
to Ghana and would be able to keep our promise to Kathryn, I

let myself relax on a whole new level. At each stoplight, people walked up and down the lanes between cars, selling everything from chewing gum to toilet paper, wiper blades to end tables, and even candies and cold water in sealed plastic bags. Many women transported goods piled in plastic tubs the size of laundry baskets on their heads with ease, often carrying a baby tied on their backs. Along the sidewalk, people sold vegetables, used clothing, new suits, and just about anything else one might want.

I was struck by the bright, jewel-colored fabrics adorned with bold patterns and symbols. Kathryn would later tell us that different ethnic groups each had their own individual cloth. The most well-known was the Kente cloth, which served as a visual representation of history and a form of written language. One particular pattern meant, "My husband is in the doghouse." When a wife went out wearing a dress in this pattern, the husband knew he was in trouble, and so did the entire neighborhood.

Kathryn arranged for her driver, Kwame, to pick us up in Accra the next morning and drive us to Cape Coast, explaining that driving ourselves would be too dangerous. I decided not to ask why, and trusted her years of experience in the country. We all took a liking to Kwame, a tall, muscular man, who seemed intimidating but had a quiet demeanor and dry sense of humor and a perfect sense of timing. On the three-hour drive from Accra to Cape Coast, Kwame did not begin many conversations, but was happy to answer our questions about the country and often interjected one-word quips into our exchanges, making us all laugh.

We spent our first few days with Kathryn getting used to our new environment. Rather than trying to keep warm as we had in Nepal, now we were just five hundred miles north of the equator and trying to keep cool with no air conditioning.

The windows of the home, though screened, were kept open for air flow, but also allowed a steady stream of ants in the kitchen and the occasional spider that proved too quick for capture. More than once, I went to bed fearful that I'd be woken in the night with those furry legs tickling my skin.

On the weekend, Kathryn and Kwame took us through the market and then to the Cape Coast slave castle. The imposing white structure served as administrative and military headquarters in colonial times. A tour led us through the rooms of the governor's palatial residence, which sat directly above a dank slave dungeon where newly enslaved Ghanaians had been held—stacked, actually, due to sheer numbers—before being loaded onto slave ships bound for the New World. The last stop of the tour was the "Door of No Return" where captives were ripped away from their homeland, loaded onto ships, and carried across an ocean to a much crueler fate, *if* they survived the journey. The glimpse into humanity's inhumanity was a wrenching experience.

On Monday, Ray was scheduled for his first day of work in Cape Coast. He showed up at the dental clinic with his approved paperwork, but was told he would not be able to work without additional hoop-jumping—specifically, a three-hour trip back to Accra, and potential weeks of waiting. Between the time the paperwork had been approved and our arrival in Ghana, a new clinic director had been appointed and had revoked his predecessor's endorsement. Kathryn was annoyed by the director's decree, but admitted that a reversal of decisions was common when new leadership took over in all levels of the African government. Instead, Kathryn set about helping us determine what to do with our newfound free time in Ghana.

"I'm sorry you went through all the trouble to get here only to have your paperwork revoked," Kathryn said. "But perhaps you can still see some of Ghana. I've asked Kwame to meet with you tomorrow to talk about the possibilities."

"It might be for the best. The malaria medication we've been taking is making us all fuzzy," Ray said, shaking his head as if to clear the cobwebs.

In Ghana, taking the medication was a necessity. Malaria is transmitted by infected mosquitos which release a parasite into one's bloodstream. The parasites then travel to the liver where they mature. After several days, mature parasites enter the bloodstream and begin infecting red blood cells. Within forty-eight to seventy-two hours, the parasites inside the red blood cells multiply, causing the infected cells to burst. The parasites continue to infect red blood cells, resulting in symptoms—ranging from chills, fever, nausea, and vomiting to life-threatening complications—occurring in two- to three-day cycles. Symptoms typically develop within ten days to four weeks following an infection.

Although I had procured enough malaria medication to see us through all of Asia, we had not needed it until we got to Ghana. Most cities we'd visited in Asia sprayed pesticides to keep the mosquito population low outside the jungles—a mixed blessing since we didn't need medication but worried about the health and environmental consequences of spraying.

The next day we walked down the road from Kathryn's house to Hans Cottage, a botel (waterside hotel) where guests could rent small boats to take on the lake. The property and all walkways were surrounded by a knee-high white picket fence that felt out of place in Africa. Kathryn had explained that crocodiles were often found near water and cautioned us to stay alert, although I couldn't imagine this short fence providing much protection from a crocodile.

We met Kwame for lunch at the botel restaurant to talk about places we might like to visit.

"We can get to Mole National Park in two days with a stop in Kumasi," Kwame said. "There is a monkey sanctuary along the way, too."

"What kind of monkeys?" RJ asked, fascinated with monkeys since our encounter in Malaysia.

Kwame turned his full attention to RJ. "I don't know the names, but a big black-and-white kind that live in the trees and another long-tailed kind that live on the ground." He smiled as RJ's eyes lit with excitement.

With a little more planning, we agreed on an ambitious four-day road trip that would take us four hundred miles north of Cape Coast to Mole National Park in the heart of Ghana.

As we finished our meals, our waitress asked if we'd like to pet a crocodile.

"What?" I asked.

I was sure I'd misheard. She couldn't have asked if we wanted to pet a crocodile—what a random question. When Kwame looked at us with wide eyes and an ever-so-slight shake of his head, I realized I'd heard correct.

"A real crocodile?" Ray asked, looking back and forth from Kwame to the waitress.

"Yes, he's right there." She pointed over the small fence at a ten-foot crocodile camouflaged in the tall grass on the bank of the lake. "I can take you to pet him."

"Um . . . I don't think so. Sounds dangerous," I said, looking to Kwame to confirm this decision.

Surely, he would tell us the truth.

"No. Too hot for him to bite," the waitress replied, before Kwame could answer.

This was one instance when I said absolutely not. I'd had so many instances of questioning whether we were safe on this trip, but I'd never felt any of us might die from our actions. I would not allow my boys to be prey. We did take pictures of the crocodile, but from a safe distance behind the fence. Our waitress, however, stood next to the beast and smiled wide as we snapped pictures of her.

"She's crazy," Kwame said, in a hushed tone, putting words to what we were all thinking.

Mole Park

Leaving the jungles of Cape Coast behind, as we drove north, the canopy and mahogany trees gave way to solitary baobabs jutting out of otherwise barren land, towering above their surroundings, giant sentinels watching over the land.

Halfway between Cape Coast and Mole National Park, we visited the Boabeng Fiema Monkey Sanctuary, home to approximately seven hundred monkeys. The monkeys lived free in the forest between two villages and were revered by their human neighbors.

Walking along the forested path, the guide kept a running commentary. "There are two types of monkeys in the forest, the Black and White Colobus monkey and the smaller Campbell's Mona monkey. The Colobus live high in the trees and the Monas live near to the ground."

Ahead of us, the path ended at a large open area, canopied by the trees. Wooden signs painted with white letters filled the open space.

"This is the graveyard for monkeys," our guide said, pointimg to the signs.

Juvenile Male, Black and White Colobus, Buried 15/3/2000.

Baby Female, Mona, Buried 1/4/2001.

"The villagers wrap every monkey in a cloth and place the body in a coffin for burial. After a member of the troop dies, the monkeys howl for hours that night. This is the signal to the people that the oldest person in one of the two villages will die," the guide continued.

"And does someone always die?" Ray asked.

"Yes. Always. The people in the villages are connected to the monkeys. They tell a story of a man who once killed a monkey. Each day, one of his relatives died until he had no one."

A quick glance at Kwame nodding confirmed the story. I wondered if the oldest person in either village feared this omen or if they embraced death, knowing it was their turn next. Would I fear death any less if I knew it was my turn?

We continued through the forest to a village where we purchased bananas to feed the monkeys.

"Can we pet them?" Ray asked.

"No. They don't let humans touch them. They will take food from you, but are wary of touch," the guide said.

As we started back, a troop of a dozen monkeys walking on all four legs, long tails held high in the air curled toward their backs, trailed behind us. Once we were under the cover of the forest, we stopped, and the guide made a clicking noise with his mouth, which the monkeys imitated. They approached our small group, the largest male leading the way.

We broke off pieces of banana and offered them to the monkeys, who snatched them from our hands and just as quickly retreated. Ray took a banana from the bunch and broke off the stem, making peeling the banana troublesome. As he was fumbling with the peel, the largest male monkey took a quick leap at Ray, bounced off his stomach and swung up to perch on his shoulder, snagging the banana along the way. He was tired of waiting for this human to open the damn thing. Ray held perfectly still, not wanting to disturb the monkey, while the boys and I took a step back and held a collective breath. I didn't know if I should worry for Ray or snap a picture. The guide had said the monkeys would not come near us, and signs throughout the forest warned about touching the animals. How aggressive was this behavior?

The guide held his palms up to Ray as if to worship him and said, "You are very blessed."

Kwame nudged me with his elbow and whispered, "Monkeys have AIDS."

I looked at Kwame and saw that he was suppressing a laugh. I was happy to have his comic relief to ease my worry.

When the monkey had eaten the entire banana, he sprang back to the ground. We laughed as we returned to our car, trailed for a time by the troop until they determined the bananas were gone. Ray had finally had his close encounter with a monkey, and I couldn't help but think there was something more at work here than a difficult banana. I felt I was now seeing an interconnectedness I hadn't paid attention to before. Was this Ray's beloved force at work? Could I manifest happiness into existence just by wishing for it?

Early the next day, we arrived at Mole National Park and checked into rooms on a bluff overlooking an elephant watering hole fifty feet below. After booking an afternoon safari, we sat on the terrace. We picked at our grilled sandwiches and *kelewele* (spicy fried plantain) watching a group of three male elephants drink and splash below, their mere presence commanding a hushed audience. I'd seen elephants before in zoos, but witnessing them in their natural habitat, we felt part of their environment.

That afternoon, as the temperatures cooled, we climbed up a ladder fastened to the back of a Jeep Cherokee and sat on makeshift benches welded to the roof. We drove around the bluff and down into the deciduous forest, leaves yellow and crumbling from lack of water. The driver stopped and motioned for us to climb down from the roof and follow him on foot through the forest. After walking a short distance, we heard branches breaking and leaves rustling in the distance. The guide pointed through the trees, not twenty yards away, to three large male elephants breaking off limbs and stripping the leaves to eat. We stood motionless, in awe of their beauty and power, watching these giant creatures use their trunks to rip the trees apart.

Continuing our tour through the forest, we saw baboons, warthogs with surprisingly cute new babies, several varieties of colorful birds, vervet monkeys, bush buck—a type of small antelope—and several crocodiles.

That night, as Ray and I lay in the dark hotel room, listening to the chirping lizards and crickets, I said, "It feels like this is our last great adventure before heading home, like it's winding down."

"Might be. I think we're all feeling like it's time to head for home," Ray said.

I thought maybe he was referring to our physical state. None of us had adjusted to the malaria medication as we'd hoped. Tyler was a walking zombie, his sleep fitful and his waking hours clouded by exhaustion. RJ and I often felt nauseous, a common side effect of the medication. Ray was so nauseous he switched to a drug that caused less nausea but instead produced intense, psychotic dreams. I knew everyone was tiring of the side effects, but I wasn't ready to be done just yet.

"Our year isn't even close to over," I said. "I'm not sure I'm ready to go back. I've enjoyed letting go of real life for a while."

Though we didn't have a timeframe in mind when we started the trip, I'd always anticipated being gone for a year.

"You don't miss home, even a little?" Ray asked.

"Yes, a little, but—" I paused to collect my thoughts, "I'm scared to go back. Probably just as scared as I was to leave."

I could feel Ray's head turn in my direction, giving me his full attention.

"What if I get back home and I shut down again?"

"I don't think things will be the same as before," Ray said.

I wished I felt as confident as he sounded. I could see how much I had changed in the six months away from my "normal" life, but in that moment, I longed for the same confidence radiating from Ray.

He let another moment of silence pass. "What are you really worried about?"

"You know how I was scared of everything when we left on the trip?" I asked.

"Yeah, you were kinda driving me crazy with all the fretting."

"Well, it's sort of like that, only the opposite. All I can think of now is every negative possibility about being at home. Just thinking about going back, I worry about work and emotions and people asking me how I am and . . . well . . . everything."

The Glitch had changed me, the way I went about my day. It had disconnected me from everyone and everything. I felt as if my brain had shut down, rewired itself, maybe to protect me, but ultimately doing more harm than good. Now after more than thirty thousand miles of travel, I finally felt like I was getting back to being myself. What if it was too soon to go home? What if I returned and changes didn't stick, and I reverted to the same patterns?

Ray shifted his arm up and pulled me close. I knew we still had a bit of time. We would spend a few weeks touring Spain, eventually making our way to Germany and the Ramstein military base to catch a Space-A flight back to the US. Lying in the dark, with Ray's arm around me, I realized I had to spend our remaining days preparing to go back. This escape was never intended to be permanent.

We spent a quiet day riding back to Cape Coast. In between cat naps, I looked out the window as we passed villages of small, one-room mud huts, with no source of water anywhere in sight. Uninhabited stretches were marked by termite mounds more than ten feet tall, hundreds of them as far as we could see. I was thankful to have Kwame, a man of few words, in charge of driving.

The day after returning to Cape Coast, RJ woke in the night and threw up and was running a high fever. When Kathryn woke, I told her of RJ's symptoms. I imagined he was just having a reaction to the malaria medication. Kathryn was not convinced. She picked up her phone and called Kwame.

"Kwame will be here shortly to take RJ right to the clinic. I'll call the doctor to tell them you're on your way," Kathryn said. "You don't mess around with fevers and vomiting in Africa."

I hadn't thought RJ's illness was serious, but Kathryn's tone of voice scared me. Was this malaria, despite the drugs we'd been taking? Only a day before, the worst thing I could think of had been my return to old habits once back home. But now my mind jumped to the worst-case scenario. Losing RJ to a tropical illness—I didn't believe I could recover from that.

I rushed around to get RJ's vaccination history prepared for Ray to show the doctor at the clinic. When Kwame arrived, I looked RJ in the eyes one more time, willing him to be alright, before sending him off with Ray to the clinic. I was not a villager who tied my existence to a troop of monkeys, who could know when death was approaching. I couldn't tell if he had a tummy bug or something more serious, but I tried to force myself to believe in the former, as if my maternal instinct might make the outcome true.

At the clinic, RJ had blood drawn, and thirty minutes later, he was back with us at Kathryn's. "It was so fast," Ray said. "We got in, had blood taken, and less than fifteen minutes later, the doctor was back with the results. That would have taken two days back in the States."

RJ had been cleared for malaria, typhoid, and yellow fever. The doctor pronounced he had a food bug, an acute illness, or a reaction to the malaria medication. Nothing more serious than that. I was flooded with relief upon hearing the news.

"They have to act fast here with malaria to get it under control as soon as possible," Kathryn explained.

Within a day or two, RJ had improved but he still looked pale, his eyes sunken. His appetite did not rebound, either. I was glad to say goodbye to Ghana. I had convinced myself that if we could just get out of Africa, RJ would be better.

Days of Travel: 170
Miles Logged: 33,698

READY OR NOT

Madrid, Spain

We hadn't planned to stop in Spain, but when Ray's dental volunteer gig was cancelled in Ghana, we had to find a way back to Europe and American military bases. Spain was the cheapest destination for short notice flights from Africa.

From the moment we arrived in Madrid, our world turned upside down again, or maybe rightside up. For the first time in six months, we were no longer the centers of attention. We were not gawked at every second, or poked, prodded, or scammed. We arrived at the airport like everyone else, and once through the airport maze to Arrivals, stood in an orderly line to rent a car. No one hurdled over us to be first to the counter. The shift was immediate, and stunning. We were in control of our own destinies, and no longer had to rely on a taxi driver or a bus to get us to our destination.

Driving in our rented car through the city, we inhaled the clean air and admired the pollution-free, brilliant blue sky. Once-typical comforts of home were now exciting discoveries. We ate meals indoors, at restaurants with windows. Our hotel had electricity and heat throughout the day. Traffic obeyed a set of organized rules we understood, and we no longer felt in danger when crossing the street. No one paid us much attention. We had returned to anonymity, and I felt a certain relief.

Had we started our trip in Spain, I might not have enjoyed the country quite so much. But having lived for months without the comforts we were accustomed to in the US, Spain felt like a return to a combination of privilege and normalcy. I saw how much we had taken for granted in our daily lives before the trip.

After a day of sightseeing, we followed the hotel's recommendation of El Tigre Tapas Bar for dinner. With the purchase of four drinks—two sangrias and two sodas—we were served four plates of delicious finger foods. Chorizo and manchego cheese, olives, *patatas bravas* (fried potatoes with a spicy sauce), and grilled bread with olive oil and salt. We received an even better four-plate serving with another round of drinks, including *tortilla Española* (Spanish omelet), *croquetas de jamon* (ham croquettes), and a variety of *toastas* (mini, crisp toast) with savory toppings. A third drink would result in the best tapas, but our appetites were no match for El Tigre.

"You know what I like best about Spain?" I said to no one in particular as I enjoyed the bites.

"The food?" Tyler said, his words mumbled through a mouthful.

I smiled at my boy, so present in the moment. "I love being anonymous. No one is staring at us, no one even knows we're Americans," I spread my arms to include everyone in the room. "As long as we don't speak, no one even looks twice at us. We blend in."

"That's the part I don't like," Ray said. "I felt like a rock star in Asia. When we walked into a room, every head turned our way, people whispered, asked to take pictures with us. Every time I signed my name on a receipt, it was like I was giving the waitress my autograph and I signed with a little more flair than normal."

"I like not towering over everyone," Tyler added.

"What do you like about Spain, RJ?" I asked.

RJ shrugged. At that moment, he couldn't find the words to tell us what he liked. I looked to see if he was just thinking about the question but saw something more. My instincts told me he didn't feel well, even if his appetite indicated otherwise.

Granada

With no remaining volunteer obligations, we took our time wandering, driving where we pleased, stopping in towns when something caught our attention, lingering when we didn't feel like moving on. Eventually we wound up in Granada, south of Madrid and close to the Alboran Sea.

I'd always wanted to visit the Alhambra—a fortress that became a palace—built on the hill above Granada. Like the temples of Ankor Wat, this was a place I'd read about extensively, each description making me fall in love with this magical structure. Even the name "Alhambra" had a mysterious source, perhaps originating from Muslim storytellers who spoke about the construction "under the light of torches."

The site of the Alhambra originally held Roman fortification. When Islamic Arabs (Moors) from North Africa invaded Spain in the eighth century and replaced Christian rulers, the fortress was constructed on the remains of the original fortification. The Islamic architecture dates from the Moorish occupation before Ferdinand and Isabella's (Christian) armies forced them out. After the expulsion of the Moors from the Iberian Peninsula, the site was converted to a royal palace.

I tried to impress upon RJ and Tyler the depth of history this palace held. "We're exploring the place where Christopher Columbus received royal endorsement for his expedition!"

My excitement was met with only a nod and "okay." I knew that in years to come, the boys would gain a better understanding of how they would never encounter a place with such history and longevity in their own country and how special this place was.

No detail was overlooked in the Alhambra. Each pebble in every walkway fell into a pattern, every wall decorated, every ceiling tiled with mosaics of complicated mathematical configurations or carved precisely with Arabic inscriptions manipulated into geometrical designs. Even the hedges and bushes were sculpted into perfect unison with one another. Column arcades, fountains with running water, and reflecting pools dominated open areas, adding to the aesthetic and filling the complex with the soothing sound of running water. The grounds were planted with roses, oranges, and myrtles, and were home to flocks of nightingales.

What I found most fascinating about this complex was that each subsequent ruler did not tear down existing structures and build new ones, but rather added to the structure, leaving the prior occupant's decorations intact, each new section following the theme of "paradise on Earth." What did these cultures know that ours seems to have forgotten? To see the beauty in someone else's creation and build upon it, rather than tear it down.

Most of the buildings opened onto a central court. The complex reached its present size by the gradual addition of new buildings of varying dimensions around this court and connected to one another by smaller rooms and passages. In every case, the exterior was left plain and austere.

After several hours of roaming through the Alhambra, we walked down the hill through the city streets on the way to the hotel, all of us in a state of quiet awe. This was a different kind of beauty—the ability to be quiet with one another, not forced to speak, but comfortable in our silence.

Walking along and thinking about the Alhambra, I reminded myself I could build a life without tearing myself apart. Even once I returned home, I could use the tools I'd learned on this trip to continue squaring myself up.

"How about dinner?" Ray asked, as we neared our hotel.

"Definitely, I'm starving," Ty said. "Let's find another tapas place."

"No," said RJ. His pallid tone and heavy eyelids made subsequent questions unnecessary.

I placed my hand on RJ's head and found he was running a fever.

"I'll take RJ to the hotel while you go in search of dinner," I told Ray. "Bring me something yummy."

He agreed, and we split ways.

As soon as RJ and I returned to the hotel, he was up and racing for the toilet to throw up. Although I was worried about RJ, I was secure in knowing we were in a nation with modern medicine and hospitals. I knew we would be well taken care of should we need help.

That evening, Ray and I plotted a course to get us to Germany where we stood the best chance of catching a flight back to the US. Our route would take us up the coast of Spain, through the cities of Alicante, Valencia, and, finally, Barcelona. From there, we would fly to Zurich, Switzerland, then take a train over the border for the remainder of the trip into Ramstein, Germany, home to the headquarters for the United States Air Forces in Europe, Air Forces Africa, and NATO Allied Air Command.

Valencia

After a few days, when RJ appeared to be on the mend and felt well enough to travel, we continued meandering through Spain, visiting Alicante and then Valencia, the third largest city in Spain. One of our primary goals on this stop was to satisfy Tyler's desire to catch a professional soccer game. Valencia happened to have a game that fit with our schedule—Valencia vs. Bilbao.

When the day for the big game arrived, we ate a small lunch and walked to the stadium.

"I don't want to go," RJ said.

"What? Why not?" Ray asked. But one look at RJ and this time we both knew he was sick again.

"I'll take him back to the hotel." I said to Ray. "And I'll try to find a clinic, too."

I was reminded of the cyclical nature of malaria, and I was starting to have doubts about the blood test in Ghana.

"See what you can find," Ray said. "We can take him in this afternoon or tomorrow if he's still bad."

Ray and Ty set off to the game while RJ and I returned to the hotel. As soon as we got back to the room, he was again racing for the bathroom. After getting him settled, I went to the front desk and asked about clinics in the area. The front desk clerk understood through the Spanish-English language barrier that my son was sick. She indicated she would call a doctor to come to the hotel.

Twenty minutes later, three medics—one doctor and two nurses—came to our room and poked and prodded RJ, taking his blood pressure, blood oxygen level, and temperature. The problem with this visit was that all three women had minimal English skills, and my Spanish was elementary at best. But we figured out that if they spoke small Spanish words mixed with a little English, and I spoke small English words mixed with a little Spanish, we could get to a place where we understood one another.

The nurse who had the best English asked me about RJ's illness. "When begin?"

"Two weeks ago, in Ghana," I said, holding up two fingers.

"Africa?" she asked, with a look of great concern.

"*Sí*," I answered.

"Where you travel?" she asked.

"Africa, India, Nepal, and *mucho* countries in Southeast Asia," I answered.

Her look of concern morphed into scorn as she rattled off my explanation to the others, too fast for me to comprehend any words except India, Africa, and "*irresponsable.*" I could tell by their pinched eyebrows and tight mouths that none of them approved of my gallivanting around the globe with my child. I couldn't help but be reminded of the days with my mother and enduring her judgment of my actions, but I put this out of my mind; this was about RJ, not about me and Mom.

After twenty more minutes of broken English and Spanish conversation, I told them that RJ had been tested for malaria and typhoid in Ghana, and that both tests were negative. The medics concluded his sickness was merely a tummy bug and would pass in a day or two. Before they left our hotel room, however, they let me know how irresponsible I was being by taking my child to dangerous places like Africa and India. I shut the door behind them, glad to be finished with their judgmental attitudes. I had no room for their scorn.

When Ray and I talked later that evening, I told him about the encounter.

"What did you say?" he asked.

"Well, I didn't say anything. They wouldn't have understood, anyway. But what I wanted to say was 'fuck you.' I have dreamed and worked and planned for years to create this opportunity for my family. I have shown my children places other kids their age only read about. Who were they to judge me?"

I could feel a flush spreading over my cheeks as my voice grew louder. "My kids have seen places and eaten foods and had experiences and adventures that will stay with them for their entire lives. We have a bond many parents will never have. Ever. I feel closer to my boys than I ever was with my parents."

I paused for a moment to catch my breath as Ray just sat back and listened. "And think of all the times in their lives when they will see something on TV or read something in a book or hear of an experience and say, 'Oh yeah, I've been there,' or 'I've done that.' This trip will stir feelings in them forever. It will for all of us. I am not irresponsible. I am a great mother."

"Did you hear what you said?" Ray asked.

"What?" I asked, worn out from my tirade.

"You said, 'I am a great mother,'" he answered. "You *are* a great mother, Lis. For whatever was lacking in your relationship with your mom, you have never let that cloud your relationship with RJ and Ty."

I turned to look at Ray, his eyes bright, his lips a crooked smile. I had not only said the words, but I truly believed them. I felt confident and powerful, as if the essence of the woman I thought I'd lost had slammed back into my body. I knew, without a doubt, who I was. The time had come for me to trust myself completely and let go of the judgments that had long made me forget myself. Grieve for the loss of loved ones, but not for a past I couldn't change.

Barcelona

RJ's tummy bug again cleared up in a couple of days and we continued our road trip to Barcelona, our last stop in Spain. Trying to remain cautious with RJ and not wanting to tax his energy, we took short walking trips around the city and made sure to get plenty of rest in the afternoons. We toured a Picasso museum and a chocolate factory. We took a short day-trip to Figueres, an hour and a half away, and visited the Salvador Dalí museum.

One of our most memorable stops in Barcelona was to a tree-lined plaza in the middle of *La Rambla*—a pedestrian walkway stretching through the middle of the city. At one end of the plaza sat a large, round fountain with statues of half-naked women standing in provocative poses surrounding the pool. I imagined these figures might have elicited giggles and embarrassment from my boys seven months earlier, but on this day, there was no reaction.

"Do you think they're appreciating the beauty of the sculptures?" Ray whispered, as we watched the boys study the fountain.

"I'd like to think so, but I'm guessing they are looking at their boobs," I said, and we laughed together.

Throughout the plaza, hundreds of pigeons strutted about, pecking the ground. Vendors lined the walkway selling bird seed, and people of all ages stood and fed the pigeons. Ray and the boys wasted no time in joining the frenzy. The birds were used to being fed by humans and did not hesitate to fly onto Tyler's outstretched arms or perch on RJ's shoulder. Tyler created a game by enticing about six birds onto his arms, sidling up to Ray, waving his arms, and yelling "Pigeon attack!" The birds fluttered around Ray's face in a winged cacophony before settling on the ground again.

On our last day, as we prepared to go on a tour of La Sagrada Familia, Antonio Gaudi's magnum opus, I sipped my coffee and opened my laptop to see what was new in the world. Messages populated my inbox. I spotted one from an unfamiliar name, with a subject of "Cleide," my girlfriend with whom I had traveled in my early twenties. I knew in an instant this message would bring bad news.

Although Cleide and I had rarely seen each other in the years after my marriage and during her simultaneous move to the East Coast, we often held marathon phone conversations to catch up on each other's lives. When she was diagnosed with uterine cancer, she moved to San Francisco to get treatment at one of the best cancer centers in the country. Ray and I traveled to see her before our trip, knowing we might not have the opportunity again. I could tell by her gaunt appearance that she was declining, but over our breakfast, she said, "You never know, I might surprise you and show up somewhere on your trip." I had been holding out hope she might do just that.

But now, looking at the e-mail, my hope disappeared. I steadied myself, and not just for the sad news about Cleide. Terror seized my heart. I did not want to fall apart and return to the clutches of The Glitch.

I squeezed my hands tight, released them, and clicked to open the e-mail.

> *Hello Lisa,*
> *My name is Cassio. I am Cleide's older brother from Vancouver. I am sad to inform you that Cleide passed away yesterday . . . .*

"Oh my gosh, Ray. Cleide's gone," I said, my voice catching, and tears welling in my eyes.

He stopped what he was doing and walked over to me. "I'm sorry to hear that, Lisa," he said, wrapping his arms around me. "I'm glad we got to see her."

I blew my nose and wiped my eyes. I sat stunned for a moment, waiting to dissolve and lose my grip, but there was only a quiet sense of peace, like the feeling I found in the monastery in Nepal.

"Are you okay to go today?" Ray asked.

I exhaled and looked at myself in the mirror. "Yeah. I think I'll be okay," I said. "This trip to the cathedral might be just what I need."

I wiped my eyes again, steadying myself. Ray took my hand, and we went to gather the boys.

As we walked the few blocks from our hotel to the cathedral, Tyler asked, "Are we really going to see another church?"

"Sort of, the Sagrada Familia is a basilica," I said.

"What's the difference?" he asked.

"A cathedral is home to a bishop. A basilica is a church with certain privileges, but the Pope must designate a basilica," I answered, the facts helping to keep me in the present moment.

"I don't understand," Ty replied.

"Me neither. I'm not sure what the privileges are, but basilicas are rare," I said.

On any other day I might have googled the answer and said more, but this was all I could come up with. My mind was focused on Cleide. She had been my first travel companion, a woman who was fluent in five languages and who'd introduced me to new places. I could imagine us visiting the basilica together, the rarity of the building reflecting the specialness of our long-lasting friendship.

While waiting for the doors to open, we walked around the building. I admired the exterior, adorned with all kinds of sculptures—snails, turtles, lizards, and snakes crawling up the pillars, life-size knights on horseback, cubist-style depictions of Jesus hanging from a cross, towering columns in mosaic tile, huge sections of wall adorned in art deco stucco designs, and disciples, angels, and trumpeters in Romanesque-style. Everywhere I looked there was something different to see.

I read a sign telling the facts about the basilica's history. Construction of La Sagrada Familia started in 1882, and when Gaudi died in 1926, the project was less than a quarter complete. Large portions of the building were still under construction, and it is projected the building will not be completed until 2026, a hundred years after Gaudi's death. When finished, La Sagrada Familia will have taken longer to build than the Egyptian Pyramids, and will be the tallest church building in the world with eighteen towers—twelve representing the apostles, four evangelists, one for the Virgin Mary, and the last representing Jesus. During our visit, only eight of the eighteen towers were complete.

Once inside, the detail and beauty of the architecture left me speechless. I stared up in wonder. The pillars started off large at the base, gradually twisting and tapering as they ascended. Then they branched out in all directions. The vaulted ceiling and branched pillars, along with the soft light coming through stained glass windows, made me feel as if I was walking in a forest. The openness of the limbs allowed for natural light to stream from skylights between the branches. At the base of each pillar sat a tortoise and a turtle, representing the Earth and the sea.

All around me I felt the same wide-eyed, open-mouthed sense of wonder coming from the crowd. Many people dabbed at their eyes and wiped their noses. Some embraced. My eyes clouded with tears as I let the emotion fill my chest.

"Are you okay, Mom?" Tyler asked.

"Yes, I'm just sad," I said, as I dug for a tissue in my purse.

"Why?" RJ asked.

"My friend Cleide died yesterday."

"Did we ever meet her?" Tyler asked.

"No, you never did." I looked up into the stone forest. "She was the first person I traveled extensively with. So many of our conversations centered on places we'd been or places we dreamed of going. She had hoped to meet us along the way on our trip, but she was too ill. I'm just sad she's gone."

Ray walked over and held me in a firm embrace as my tears continued to flow. I realized in that moment I was allowing myself a long-overdue experience of grief. As Ray held me, and my sons stood by my side, sharing their presence, I thought back on each death I'd lived through.

While traveling, I'd let go of many of my burdens, yet I wasn't sure if I'd ever let myself get to a place of completion with my losses. But standing in this spiritual place, filled with so many symbols of life and death, I could feel the complete circle. Death was unavoidable. And beautiful, too, in its own way, in its own place. I could see now that the villagers in Ghana, so tied to the life-and-death link between the monkeys and the elders, were much more aware of this connection. As my tears fell, I chose to believe that neither group feared death, but accepted it as a part of life, knowing with grace when their time on Earth was up.

After a few moments, RJ and Tyler joined in the group hug, making me cry harder still. A part of me knew in this moment, maybe for the first time, I was letting them see my emotional response to death. I was teaching my sons about grief and love and loss, how they are woven tightly together—none fully experienced without the others. And standing in the middle of La

Sagrada Familia, wrapped in the arms of my husband and sons, I saw a family connected, truly squared up for the first time.

"Hey Lis, I know you love cathedrals, but this is a little over the top," Ray whispered in my ear.

"Basilica," I sniffled.

I looked at him and we all started giggling. I wiped away the tears and felt lighter.

"What's next?" he asked.

"Well, we still have to go up the tower and look at the view." I smiled at Ray, and then RJ and Tyler to reassure them that I would be okay.

The four of us took an elevator to the top of the Passion tower, where, at two hundred and fifty feet above street level, we saw the progress of the construction from an aerial perspective. We looked out over the city of Barcelona, white buildings with red-tiled roofs set against a brilliant blue sky, a mix of old and modern.

I let the wonder of this place lift my spirits. Gaudi was on to something when he envisioned a church with architecture lending an invitation to prayer. Although the moment of grief had been brief, my heart was at ease. That's how it works, I thought to myself. There comes a moment, even after years and years, when it is time to let go of everything you held on to. Even, someday, life itself.

I looked at Ray and my boys and knew each of us was in our own cycle, one that could end at any time. Trying to hold it back was useless. There is no holding back death when the moment comes. The only thing I had control over was how I approached each day and how present I was in each moment. Perhaps by being present, when my time finally came, I would hear the monkeys howling and I would be prepared to go forward into the unknown, with courage and an open heart.

Ray put his arm around me. "Well, where do you think we should go next?"

I thought about how far we'd come—215 days, 13 countries, 70-plus cities, and almost 50,000 miles—and how I'd changed. I was exactly who I needed to be, a stable, steady wall in my family stupa. And that's where my responsibility ended. I was done looking in the rearview mirror wishing for my life to be different, and trying to live up to someone else's ideals. It was time for me to focus on the life ahead of me, to be a constant support for my husband and sons. Spouses and children would be added over the years, but we four, the original square and stable foundation, would serve as the pattern for generations to follow.

I took one last look at the city sprawling out before us, then the unfinished cathedral, and finally, at Ray, RJ and Tyler.

"I think I'm ready to go home."

Days Left to Travel: Indeterminable
Miles to be Logged: Infinite

ACKNOWLEDGMENTS

Square Up was the not the first book I thought I'd write, but it's the first story that wanted to be told, and would not have come to life without an amazing group of writers and mentors cheering me on.

I took a stab at writing about our trip but realized after a first draft that it was terrible! And just when I wasn't sure where to turn, I was invited to a weekend retreat for memoir writers where I met Cami Ostman, founder of The Narrative Project. I joined her nine-month program and was able to revise my memoir with her guidance and the help of my small writing group and coach, Rebecca Mabanglo-Mayor. I spent the next two years in weekly meetings at Starbucks with my writing partner, Lorinda Boyer, where we helped each other find the words and confidence to tell our stories.

I was welcomed into the Red Wheelbarrow Writers by Laura Kalpakian, who invited me knowing nothing more about me than I was writing a little something. In truth, I was feeling completely out of place and supposed my dream of writing a book might never happen. Through Red Wheelbarrow, I was connected with a community of writers, joined critique groups, and further honed my story.

And just when I thought I was done writing, I sent my manuscript to Laurel Leigh for developmental editing. With kind words, a relentless finger on the delete key, and a magical capacity to see writing patterns, Laurel made the necessary cuts I couldn't do on my own and directed my focus to what was important to the story. And then came Dana Tye Rally, who cleaned up my (many) mistakes and brought further clarity to my words.

To all the members of my critique groups, those who read early drafts, and those on the sidelines who cheered me on even when I felt like giving up—Linda Morrow, Cheryl Stritzel McCarthy, Kathie Tupper, Lorinda Boyer, Priscilla Sharrow, Marian Exall, Linda Lambert, Amory Peck, Heather Lea, Steve and Lee Whitney—thank you.

Most of all, thanks to my husband, Ray, and my sons, RJ and Tyler, whose belief in me never wavers.

ABOUT THE AUTHOR

Lisa Dailey is an avid traveler and writer. In her time abroad, she unearthed new ways of looking at her life through her discoveries in remote corners of the world, and she continues to enrich her life through travel. She is currently working on a recipe anthology, as well as her first work of fiction. A native Montanan, Lisa now makes her home by the ocean in Bellingham, Washington, but returns to her roots every summer for a healthy dose of mountains and Big Sky. Lisa is the owner of Silent Sidekick and Sidekick Press, where she helps guide authors through their publishing journey.

CPSIA information can be obtained
at www.ICGtesting.com
Printed in the USA
LVHW040212120522
718517LV00008B/1086